COOKIES
BROWNIES
& BARS

Ottenheimer Publishers, Inc.

German Choc. Saucepan Brownies
P.64 (Frosting)

PUBLISHER	Sally Peters
PUBLICATION MANAGER	William Monn
ASSOCIATE EDITOR	Elaine Christiansen
SENIOR FOOD EDITOR	Jackie Sheehan
TEST KITCHEN COORDINATOR	Pat Peterson
CIRCULATION SPECIALIST	Karen Goodsell
PUBLICATION SECRETARY	Mary Memorich
FOOD EDITOR	Grace Wells
FOOD STYLIST	Barb Standal
FOOD STYLIST'S ASSISTANTS	Grace Wells, Susanne Mattison
CONTRIBUTING EDITOR	Grace Wells
CONSULTING EDITOR	Diane B. Anderson
HOME ECONOMISTS	Pillsbury Publications
NUTRITION INFORMATION	Pillsbury Technology
DESIGN, PRODUCTION	Sheila Chin Morris
PHOTOGRAPHY	Glenn Peterson, Inc., Photographers

Cover Photo: Poppin' Fresh Double Decker Cookies p. 6.

distributed by Wholesale Warehousing Industries, Inc.,
250 Granton Drive, Richmond Hill, Ontario, Canada, L4B 1H7.

CLASSIC® Pillsbury COOKBOOKS

Cookies Brownies & Bars

4
Cookies
Delight in this delectable collection.

48
Brownies
Tantalize with these irresistible creations!

66
Bars
Rely on bars for versatility and flavor.

Chocolaty
Caramel Pecan
Bars p. 68

ppin Fresh™
uble Decker
Cookies p. 6

Cranberry
and Orange
Pinwheels
p. 40

EDITOR'S Pillsbury NOTEBOOK

Cookies Brownies & Bars

There is nothing more tempting than oven fresh cookies, brownies or bars.

Let's Reminisce . . .

Everybody loves them, anyone can bake them and nothing says lovin' from the oven more completely than cookies, brownies and bars! Thoughts of these hand-held goodies often bring back treasured memories of baking cookies as a family project. And what could be more pleasant than the aroma of fragrant cookies baking in a cozy kitchen.

All-Occasion Treats . . .

In this cookbook, you'll find our newest and most tempting cookie collection. We've included recipes for:

✔ Snacking or packing.

✔ Potlucks or school activities.

✔ Family get-togethers.

✔ Parties and special occasions.

Look for several Halloween ideas that will inspire you to have great fun with goblins of all ages.

Whether you're in the mood for an old family favorite or a unique new idea, you're sure to find it here.

Ease of Preparation . . .

Cookies, brownies and bars lend themselves to easy preparation methods. In this special collection, you'll find

**Fun to make!
Fun to eat!
Andy's Dyno
S'mores p. 15**

recipes for tasty drop cookies, convenient refrigerator cookies and spread-in-the-pan bar cookies. Recipes using purchased cookies and other convenience products also make preparation a breeze. We've included recipes for cut-out cookies, filled cookies and more elaborate brownies and bars. There is even a recipe for a cookie pizza! So whether you want to "fix-it-fast" or "make-it-from-scratch," there's a recipe for you.

lanning to send me cookies to a loved one? We ggest Chocolate Pixies p. 24.

How to Ship . . .

Many of the cookies, brownies and bars are suitable for shipping to friends and relatives out of town. We know that when you send treats to someone, it is important to know that they will arrive at their destination in tip-top shape. We've included instructions for packing and shipping in a Cook's Note on page 63 that should help make it all easier to do.

Healthful Ingredients . . .

Many recipes were created with healthier additions in mind. Preparing sweet treats with healthful ingredients can boost fiber, vitamins and minerals. We feel that these special ingredients also increase flavor and add to texture and appearance. Healthful additions to look for in this book include:

- ✔ Rolled oats, granola and other cereals
- ✔ Whole wheat flour
- ✔ Dried fruits
- ✔ Nuts
- ✔ Buttermilk and yogurt
- ✔ Fresh fruits and vegetables
- ✔ Peanut butter and peanuts
- ✔ Molasses and honey

Kids in the Kitchen . . .

For cooks-in-training, cookies, brownies and bars are perfect. Easy-to-make recipes with few ingredients are ideal for beginners. This month's Classic Know-How™ on page 12 describes making **Chocolate Chunk Cookies** with step-by-step photos and instructions.

The perfect treat for the season! Molasses Jack-O-Lantern Cookies p. 45

COOKIES

Delight in this delectable collection.

Crisp, chewy, soft or cake-like, cookies are always welcome as a sweet treat, dessert or gift. In **Giant Peanut Butter Zebra Cookies**, we've combined Pillsbury Refrigerated Cookie Dough, creamy candies and a yummy chocolate drizzle to create filled cookies that are destined to become a family favorite. Whimsical **Chocolate Raisin Smile Cookies** are sure to put a smile on anyone's face with their frosted happy faces. **Almond Kiss Cookies**, a favorite with our tasters, are so-o-o pretty and so-o-o easy to make!

Pictured:
POPPIN' FRESH™ DOUBLE DECKER COOKIES
Page 6

Make these delightful, flavor-filled cookies in your choice of sizes. Bite-sized cookies are ideal for younger children, while larger cookies are better suited for bigger "kids."

POPPIN' FRESH™ DOUBLE DECKER COOKIES

(pictured on p. 4 and cover)

1 (20-oz.) pkg. Pillsbury's BEST®
  Refrigerated Peanut Butter
  Cookies
  Sugar
1 (20-oz.) pkg. Pillsbury's BEST®
  Refrigerated Chocolate Chip
  Cookies
1 can Pillsbury Chocolate
  Frosting Supreme™
½ cup creamy peanut butter

Heat oven to 350°F. Divide peanut butter cookie dough into 36 equal pieces, rolling each into a ball. Place 2 inches apart on ungreased cookie sheets. Using fork dipped in sugar, flatten each ball slightly in crisscross pattern.

Bake at 350°F. for 8 to 11 minutes or until light golden brown. Immediately remove from cookie sheets. Repeat with chocolate chip cookie dough.

In small bowl, combine frosting and peanut butter; blend well. Spread about 1 tablespoonful frosting mixture on bottom of each peanut butter cookie; top each with one chocolate chip cookie, pressing gently. Store in refrigerator.
3 dozen sandwich cookies.

NUTRITION INFORMATION

SERVING SIZE: 1 COOKIE		PERCENT U.S. RDA PER SERVING	
CALORIES	200	PROTEIN	4%
PROTEIN	3 g	VITAMIN A	*
CARBOHYDRATE	26 g	VITAMIN C	*
FAT	10 g	THIAMINE	2%
CHOLESTEROL	7 mg	RIBOFLAVIN	4%
SODIUM	170 mg	NIACIN	6%
POTASSIUM	105 mg	CALCIUM	*
		IRON	2%

* Contains less than 2% of the U.S. RDA of this nutrient.

VARIATION: MINI-DOUBLE DECKER COOKIES: Divide each roll of cookie dough into 54 pieces. Prepare as directed above. Bake at 350°F. for 8 to 11 minutes. Continue as directed above, using about 1 teaspoonful frosting mixture for each cookie sandwich.
4½ dozen sandwich cookies.

Using Pillsbury Refrigerated Cookie Dough makes it easy to create colorful, tasty cookies. What could be easier than slicing cookie dough and adding flavored candies? Adults can slice the cookie dough and children can choose their favorite gumdrop flavors.

CONFETTI SUGAR COOKIES

1 (20-oz.) pkg. Pillsbury's BEST®
  Refrigerated Sugar Cookies
45 small spiced gumdrop
  candies, cut in half

Heat oven to 350°F. Cut cookie dough into about thirty ¼-inch thick slices. Place 2 inches apart on ungreased cookie sheets. Top each slice with 3 gumdrop halves, pressing lightly into dough.

Bake at 350°F. for 8 to 11 minutes or until golden brown. Cool 1 minute; remove from cookie sheets.
30 cookies.

NUTRITION INFORMATION

SERVING SIZE: 1 COOKIE		PERCENT U.S. RDA PER SERVING	
CALORIES	90	PROTEIN	*
PROTEIN	1 g	VITAMIN A	*
CARBOHYDRATE	16 g	VITAMIN C	*
FAT	3 g	THIAMINE	2%
CHOLESTEROL	2 mg	RIBOFLAVIN	*
SODIUM	80 mg	NIACIN	2%
POTASSIUM	15 mg	CALCIUM	*
		IRON	2%

* Contains less than 2% of the U.S. RDA of this nutrient.

Children will enjoy making these chunky, chewy cookies and munching on the extra candy and peanuts!

PEANUT AND CANDY JUMBLES

1 cup firmly packed brown
   sugar
½ cup margarine or butter,
   softened
½ cup creamy peanut butter
1 tablespoon vanilla
1 egg
1 cup Pillsbury's BEST® All
   Purpose or Unbleached
   Flour
½ cup Pillsbury's BEST® Whole
   Wheat Flour
1 teaspoon baking soda
¾ cup salted peanuts
¾ cup candy-coated chocolate
   pieces

Heat oven to 375°F. In large bowl, beat brown sugar, margarine and peanut butter until light and fluffy. Add vanilla and egg; blend well. Lightly spoon flour into measuring cup; level off. Stir in all purpose flour, whole wheat flour and baking soda; mix well. Stir in peanuts and candy-coated chocolate pieces. Drop dough by rounded tablespoonfuls 2 inches apart onto ungreased cookie sheets.

Bake at 375°F. for 6 to 10 minutes or until light golden brown. Immediately remove from cookie sheets. Cool completely. 3 dozen cookies.

HIGH ALTITUDE – Above 3500 Feet: Decrease brown sugar to ¾ cup. Bake as directed above.

NUTRITION INFORMATION

SERVING SIZE: 1 COOKIE		PERCENT U.S. RDA PER SERVING	
CALORIES	130	PROTEIN	4%
PROTEIN	3 g	VITAMIN A	2%
CARBOHYDRATE	14 g	VITAMIN C	*
FAT	7 g	THIAMINE	2%
CHOLESTEROL	6 mg	RIBOFLAVIN	2%
SODIUM	105 mg	NIACIN	6%
POTASSIUM	80 mg	CALCIUM	*
		IRON	2%

* Contains less than 2% of the U.S. RDA of this nutrient.

Cook's Note

COOKIE SHEETS

The type of cookie sheet used to bake cookies can affect their color, shape and texture. Shiny, heavy-gauge aluminum cookie sheets with very low sides or no sides at all will produce the best all-around cookies. Dark cookie sheets may absorb heat and cause overbrowning on the bottoms of cookies. Non-stick cookie sheets work well if they are not too dark.

Insulated cookie sheets have become available and are becoming very popular. They are made from two sheets of aluminum separated by an insulating layer of air. In general, these cookie sheets are acceptable when two factors are taken into consideration.
(1) Cookies will not brown on the bottom when baked on insulated cookie sheets. For many cookies, this is desirable, but it can make doneness difficult to determine.
(2) Cookies will bake just slightly longer on an insulated baking sheet. We tested our cookie recipes on both kinds of cookie sheets, so this extra time is included in the range given for baking times.

For a special occasion, these pretty cookies can be made ahead and frozen. Place the cookies between sheets of waxed paper in a tightly covered container and freeze them for up to six months. When ready to serve, remove them from the freezer and allow to thaw at room temperature for about two hours.

ALMOND KISS COOKIES

(pictured on right and cover)

COOKIES
½ **cup sugar**
½ **cup firmly packed brown sugar**
½ **cup margarine or butter, softened**
½ **cup shortening**
1 **teaspoon almond extract**
1 **egg**
2 **cups Pillsbury's BEST® All Purpose or Unbleached Flour**
1 **teaspoon baking soda**
¼ **teaspoon salt**
  Sugar
  About 48 almond-filled milk chocolate candy kisses

GLAZE
¼ **cup seedless raspberry preserves or red currant jelly**
¼ **teaspoon almond extract**

In large bowl, beat sugar, brown sugar, margarine and shortening until light and fluffy. Add 1 teaspoon almond extract and egg; blend well. Lightly spoon flour into measuring cup; level off. Stir in flour, baking soda and salt; mix well. Cover with plastic wrap; refrigerate 1 hour for easier handling.

Heat oven to 325°F. Shape dough into 1-inch balls; roll in sugar. Place 2 inches apart on ungreased cookie sheets. Bake at 325°F. for 7 to 12 minutes or until light golden brown. Immediately top each cookie with a candy kiss, pressing down gently. Remove from cookie sheets.

In small bowl, combine glaze ingredients; blend well. Drizzle over cookies. Cool completely.
4 dozen cookies.

HIGH ALTITUDE – Above 3500 Feet: No change.

NUTRITION INFORMATION

SERVING SIZE: 1 COOKIE		PERCENT U.S. RDA PER SERVING	
CALORIES	110	PROTEIN	*
PROTEIN	1 g	VITAMIN A	*
CARBOHYDRATE	13 g	VITAMIN C	*
FAT	6 g	THIAMINE	2%
CHOLESTEROL	6 mg	RIBOFLAVIN	2%
SODIUM	65 mg	NIACIN	*
POTASSIUM	35 mg	CALCIUM	*
		IRON	2%

* Contains less than 2% of the U.S. RDA of this nutrient.

Almond Kiss Cookies

Store this cookie dough in the refrigerator for up to 5 days and bake cookies as desired. Either light or dark molasses can be used to make this favorite cookie.

CRISP AND CHEWY MOLASSES COOKIES

¾ **cup sugar**
½ **cup margarine or butter, softened**
½ **cup molasses**
1 **egg**
2 **cups Pillsbury's BEST® All Purpose or Unbleached Flour**
1½ **teaspoons baking soda**
½ **teaspoon cinnamon**
¼ **teaspoon cloves**
¼ **teaspoon nutmeg**
¼ **teaspoon ginger**

In large bowl, beat sugar and margarine until light and fluffy. Add molasses and egg; blend well. Lightly spoon flour into measuring cup; level off. Stir in remaining ingredients; mix well. Cover with plastic wrap; refrigerate 30 minutes for easier handling. On waxed paper, form dough into roll 9½ inches long. Wrap in waxed paper or plastic wrap; refrigerate at least 6 hours or up to 5 days.

Heat oven to 375°F. Cut dough into ½-inch thick slices; cut each slice into fourths. Place 2 inches apart on ungreased cookie sheets. Bake at 375°F. for 6 to 10 minutes or until set. Immediately remove from cookie sheets. 5 dozen cookies.

HIGH ALTITUDE – Above 3500 Feet: Decrease sugar to ½ cup. Decrease molasses to ¼ cup. Bake as directed above.

NUTRITION INFORMATION

SERVING SIZE: 1 COOKIE		PERCENT U.S. RDA PER SERVING	
CALORIES	45	PROTEIN	*
PROTEIN	1 g	VITAMIN A	*
CARBOHYDRATE	7 g	VITAMIN C	*
FAT	2 g	THIAMINE	2%
CHOLESTEROL	4 mg	RIBOFLAVIN	*
SODIUM	50 mg	NIACIN	*
POTASSIUM	35 mg	CALCIUM	*
		IRON	2%

* Contains less than 2% of the U.S. RDA of this nutrient.

These chewy cookies have a delectable maple flavor that combines wonderfully with the dates and walnuts. Refrigerating the dough for a short time before baking the cookies makes it easier to handle.

MAPLE DATE COOKIES

1 **cup firmly packed brown sugar**
¾ **cup margarine or butter, softened**
½ **teaspoon vanilla**
½ **teaspoon maple extract**
1 **egg**
1½ **cups Pillsbury's BEST® All Purpose or Unbleached Flour**
¾ **teaspoon baking powder**
¾ **teaspoon baking soda**
¼ **teaspoon salt**
1 **cup finely chopped dates**
½ **cup chopped walnuts or pecans**

In large bowl, beat brown sugar and margarine until light and fluffy. Add vanilla, maple extract and egg; blend well. Lightly spoon flour into measuring cup; level off. Stir in flour, baking powder, baking soda and salt; mix well. Stir in dates and walnuts. Cover with plastic wrap; refrigerate 30 minutes for easier handling.

Heat oven to 350°F. Shape dough into 1-inch balls. Place 2 inches apart on ungreased cookie sheets. Bake at 350°F. for 9 to 12 minutes or until light golden brown. 5 dozen cookies.

HIGH ALTITUDE – Above 3500 Feet: Increase flour to 2 cups. Bake as directed above.

NUTRITION INFORMATION

SERVING SIZE: 1 COOKIE		PERCENT U.S. RDA PER SERVING	
CALORIES	60	PROTEIN	*
PROTEIN	1 g	VITAMIN A	2%
CARBOHYDRATE	8 g	VITAMIN C	*
FAT	3 g	THIAMINE	2%
CHOLESTEROL	4 mg	RIBOFLAVIN	*
SODIUM	55 mg	NIACIN	*
POTASSIUM	45 mg	CALCIUM	*
		IRON	*

* Contains less than 2% of the U.S. RDA of this nutrient.

The whole family will enjoy these crisp cereal cookies. They are great to pack for lunches or snacks.

RANGER CRISPIES

1 cup sugar
1 cup firmly packed brown
   sugar
½ cup margarine or butter,
   softened
⅓ cup shortening
1 teaspoon vanilla
2 eggs
2¼ cups Pillsbury's BEST® All
   Purpose or Unbleached
   Flour
1 teaspoon baking powder
1 teaspoon baking soda
1 teaspoon salt
3 cups crisp rice cereal

Heat oven to 375°F. Lightly grease cookie sheets. In large bowl, beat sugar, brown sugar, margarine and shortening until light and fluffy. Add vanilla and eggs; blend well. Lightly spoon flour into measuring cup; level off. Stir in flour, baking powder, baking soda and salt; mix well. Stir in cereal. Drop dough by rounded teaspoonfuls 2 inches apart onto greased cookie sheets.

Bake at 375°F. for 8 to 12 minutes or until golden brown. Cool 1 minute; remove from cookie sheets. Cool completely. 5 dozen cookies.

HIGH ALTITUDE – Above 3500 Feet: Decrease baking powder and baking soda to ½ teaspoon each. Bake as directed above.

Cook's Note

SELECTING SHORTENING FOR COOKIE BAKING

Regular butter and margarine can be used interchangeably in most cookie recipes. Butter and margarine both provide good flavor and a crisp texture to cookies. Vegetable shortening produces a crunchy, more crumbly cookie without adding flavor. It is not recommended to use whipped butter, whipped margarine, tub-style soft margarine, reduced-calorie magarine or liquid margarine for cookie baking. The additional air in whipped products and a higher water content in reduced-calorie margarine may result in thin, flat cookies.

NUTRITION INFORMATION

SERVING SIZE: 1 COOKIE		PERCENT U.S. RDA PER SERVING	
CALORIES	80	PROTEIN	*
PROTEIN	1 g	VITAMIN A	2%
CARBOHYDRATE	12 g	VITAMIN C	*
FAT	3 g	THIAMINE	4%
CHOLESTEROL	7 mg	RIBOFLAVIN	2%
SODIUM	95 mg	NIACIN	2%
POTASSIUM	20 mg	CALCIUM	*
		IRON	2%

* Contains less than 2% of the U.S. RDA of this nutrient.

Making Drop Cookies

So easy for kids of any age to make.

Because they are the easiest of all cookies to make, drop cookies are perfect for first-time bakers. A few simple guidelines for children to follow when baking are:

✔ Have a grown-up close by to help.
✔ Read the recipe carefully and gather together ingredients and baking utensils.
✔ Place one cookie sheet at a time on the middle oven rack.
✔ Check the cookies at the earliest baking time indicated.
✔ Always use potholders to remove cookie sheets from the oven.
✔ Let hot cookie sheets cool before putting the next batch of dough on them.

These step-by-step photo directions will help ensure successful results for young bakers.

◀ **Step 1:** In large mixer bowl, beat brown sugar, sugar, margarine and shortening until the mixture is light in color and fluffy in texture. This takes 2 to 3 minutes with an electric mixer. If you are using a wooden spoon, it will take longer. Add the egg and vanilla and beat until the mixture is smooth and creamy. The flour, baking soda and salt can be mixed in with an electric mixer or stirred in until it is completely combined. The dough will be quite stiff.

▶ **Step 2**: Using a wooden spoon, stir in the chopped chocolate and nuts until the pieces are evenly distributed.

▼ **Step 3**: To bake the cookies, drop small

amounts of cookie dough onto a cookie sheet. An easy way to do this is to use a rubber spatula and regular-sized tablespoon to spoon and drop the dough in equal-sized mounds, about 2-inches apart on the cookie sheet to allow for spreading during baking.

Delicious chunks of semi-sweet chocolate dot these easy drop cookies.

CHOCOLATE CHUNK COOKIES

(pictured below)

¾ cup firmly packed brown sugar
½ cup sugar
½ cup margarine or butter, softened
½ cup shortening
1½ teaspoons vanilla
1 egg
1¾ cups Pillsbury's BEST® All Purpose or Unbleached Flour
1 teaspoon baking soda
½ teaspoon salt
8 oz. (8 squares) semi-sweet chocolate, coarsely chopped, or 1 cup chocolate chips
1 cup chopped nuts

Heat oven to 375°F. In large bowl, beat brown sugar, sugar, margarine and shortening until light and fluffy. Add vanilla and egg; blend well. Lightly spoon flour into measuring cup; level off. Add flour, baking soda and salt; mix well. Stir in chocolate and nuts. Drop by tablespoonfuls 2 inches apart onto ungreased cookie sheets.

Bake at 375°F. for 9 to 12 minutes or until light golden brown. Cool 1 minute; remove from cookie sheets. 3 dozen cookies.

HIGH ALTITUDE - Above 3500 Feet: Increase flour to 2 cups. Bake as directed above.

NUTRITION INFORMATION

SERVING SIZE: 1 COOKIE		PERCENT U.S. RDA PER SERVING	
CALORIES	150	PROTEIN	2%
PROTEIN	2 g	VITAMIN A	2%
CARBOHYDRATE	16 g	VITAMIN C	*
FAT	10 g	THIAMINE	4%
CHOLESTEROL	6 mg	RIBOFLAVIN	2%
SODIUM	95 mg	NIACIN	2%
POTASSIUM	65 mg	CALCIUM	*
		IRON	4%

* Contains less than 2% of the U.S. RDA of this nutrient.

Chocolate Chunk Cookies

Whole wheat flour adds a slightly nutty flavor and texture to this traditional cookie. Store whole wheat flour in the refrigerator or freezer to prevent spoilage.

WHOLE WHEAT SNICKERDOODLES

1½ cups sugar
½ cup margarine or butter, softened
1 teaspoon vanilla
2 eggs
1 cup Pillsbury's BEST® All Purpose or Unbleached Flour
1 cup Pillsbury's BEST® Whole Wheat Flour
1 teaspoon cream of tartar
½ teaspoon baking soda
¼ teaspoon salt
2 tablespoons sugar
2 teaspoons cinnamon

Heat oven to 350°F. In large bowl, beat sugar and margarine until light and fluffy. Add vanilla and eggs; blend well. Lightly spoon flour into measuring cup; level off. Stir in all purpose flour, whole wheat flour, cream of tartar, baking soda and salt; mix well. Shape dough into 1-inch balls. In small bowl, combine 2 tablespoons sugar and cinnamon. Roll balls in sugar-cinnamon mixture. Place 2 inches apart on ungreased cookie sheets.

Bake at 350°F. for 10 to 14 minutes or until set. Immediately remove from cookie sheets. Cool completely. 4 to 5 dozen cookies.

HIGH ALTITUDE – Above 3500 Feet: No change.

NUTRITION INFORMATION

SERVING SIZE: 1 COOKIE		PERCENT U.S. RDA PER SERVING	
CALORIES	50	PROTEIN	*
PROTEIN	1 g	VITAMIN A	*
CARBOHYDRATE	9 g	VITAMIN C	*
FAT	2 g	THIAMINE	*
CHOLESTEROL	7 mg	RIBOFLAVIN	*
SODIUM	40 mg	NIACIN	*
POTASSIUM	15 mg	CALCIUM	*
		IRON	*

* Contains less than 2% of the U.S. RDA of this nutrient.

Andy's Dyno S'More

Part of the fun of making these quick and easy treats is counting the marshmallows and chocolate chips. Kids can choose to use all one flavor of marshmallow or a variety in their s'mores.

ANDY'S DYNO S'MORE

(pictured on left)

2 (3x3-inch) dinosaur-shaped graham crackers
7 multi-colored flavored miniature marshmallows
12 milk chocolate chips

■ MICROWAVE DIRECTIONS: Place 1 dinosaur cracker upside down on microwave-safe plate. Arrange marshmallows and chocolate chips on cracker. Place second dinosaur cracker right side up over marshmallows and chocolate chips. Microwave on HIGH for 20 to 30 seconds or until marshmallows puff. Serve warm. 1 sandwich cookie.

NUTRITION INFORMATION

SERVING SIZE: 1 COOKIE		PERCENT U.S. RDA PER SERVING	
CALORIES	100	PROTEIN	2%
PROTEIN	2 g	VITAMIN A	*
CARBOHYDRATE	18 g	VITAMIN C	*
FAT	3 g	THIAMINE	*
CHOLESTEROL	1 mg	RIBOFLAVIN	6%
SODIUM	105 mg	NIACIN	2%
POTASSIUM	80 mg	CALCIUM	2%
		IRON	2%

* Contains less than 2% of the U.S. RDA of this nutrient.

For the most intense flavor, use fresh-squeezed orange juice and freshly grated orange peel to make these special drop cookies. When grating orange peel, grate only the orange part of the peel. The white part of the peel has a bitter flavor.

FRESH ORANGE COOKIES

COOKIES

1½ cups sugar
1 cup margarine or butter, softened
1 cup dairy sour cream
2 eggs
4 cups Pillsbury's BEST® All Purpose or Unbleached Flour
1 teaspoon baking powder
1 teaspoon baking soda
½ teaspoon salt
⅔ cup orange juice
3 tablespoons grated orange peel

FROSTING

¼ cup margarine or butter, melted
2 cups powdered sugar
1 tablespoon grated orange peel
2 to 3 tablespoons orange juice

Heat oven to 375°F. In large bowl, beat sugar and 1 cup margarine until light and fluffy. Add sour cream and eggs; blend well. Lightly spoon flour into measuring cup; level off. Stir in flour and remaining cookie ingredients; mix well. Drop dough by rounded teaspoonfuls onto ungreased cookie sheets.

Bake at 375°F. for 8 to 11 minutes or until edges are light golden brown. Immediately remove from cookie sheets.

In small bowl, combine all frosting ingredients, adding enough orange juice for desired spreading consistency. Frost warm cookies. 6 dozen cookies.

HIGH ALTITUDE - Above 3500 Feet: No change.

Because of its firm chewy texture, this traditional icebox cookie is ideal for mailing. Pack the cookies snugly in rows in a firm box or metal container. If necessary, cushion cookies with crumpled waxed paper.

SPICED WHOLE WHEAT REFRIGERATOR COOKIES

½ cup sugar
½ cup firmly packed brown sugar
½ cup margarine or butter, softened
2 tablespoons water
2 teaspoons vanilla
1 egg
1¾ cups Pillsbury's BEST® Whole Wheat Flour
1 teaspoon baking powder
1 teaspoon cinnamon
½ teaspoon baking soda
¼ teaspoon salt
¼ teaspoon cloves
½ cup finely chopped pecans or walnuts

In large bowl, beat sugar, brown sugar and margarine until light and fluffy. Add water, vanilla and egg; blend well. Lightly spoon flour into measuring cup; level off. Add whole wheat flour, baking powder, cinnamon, baking soda, salt and cloves; mix well. Stir in pecans. On waxed paper, form dough into two

---

6-inch long rolls. Wrap in waxed paper; refrigerate at least 2 hours.

Heat oven to 375°F. Using sharp knife, cut dough into ¼-inch thick slices. Place 2 inches apart on ungreased cookie sheets. Bake at 375°F. for 6 to 8 minutes or until set. Cool 1 minute; remove from cookie sheets. Cool completely.
3½ dozen cookies.

HIGH ALTITUDE – Above 3500 Feet: Decrease sugar to ⅓ cup. Decrease brown sugar to ⅓ cup. Increase flour to 2 cups. Bake as directed above.

NUTRITION INFORMATION

SERVING SIZE: 1 COOKIE		PERCENT U.S. RDA PER SERVING	
CALORIES	70	PROTEIN	*
PROTEIN	1 g	VITAMIN A	*
CARBOHYDRATE	9 g	VITAMIN C	*
FAT	3 g	THIAMINE	*
CHOLESTEROL	5 mg	RIBOFLAVIN	*
SODIUM	60 mg	NIACIN	*
POTASSIUM	40 mg	CALCIUM	*
		IRON	2%

* Contains less than 2% of the U.S. RDA of this nutrient.

These unique sandwich cookies are pretty enough for a special occasion, yet easy enough to serve anytime. Using real butter produces a crispy, lacy, tender cookie.

───────────

MOLASSES CHOCOLATE LACE COOKIES

COOKIES
⅔ cup butter (do not use margarine)
⅔ cup Pillsbury's BEST® All Purpose or Unbleached Flour
2 cups quick-cooking rolled oats
1 cup sugar
¼ teaspoon salt
¼ cup milk
¼ cup molasses
1 teaspoon vanilla

FILLING
1 (11½-oz.) pkg. (2 cups) milk chocolate chips

Heat oven to 375°F. Line cookie sheets with foil. Melt butter in medium saucepan over low heat; remove from heat. Lightly spoon flour into measuring cup; level off. Stir flour and remaining cookie ingredients into melted butter; mix well. Drop by level teaspoonfuls about 3 inches apart onto foil-lined cookie sheets; spread thin with rubber spatula.

Bake at 375°F. for 5 to 7 minutes or until lacy and golden. Cool completely on cookie sheet (at least 15 minutes). Peel foil away from cookies.

Melt chocolate chips in small saucepan over low heat, stirring constantly. Spread thin layer of melted chocolate on flat side of half the cookies. Top with remaining cookies. 3½ dozen sandwich cookies.

HIGH ALTITUDE – Above 3500 Feet: No change.

NUTRITION INFORMATION

SERVING SIZE: 1 COOKIE		PERCENT U.S. RDA PER SERVING	
CALORIES	110	PROTEIN	2%
PROTEIN	1 g	VITAMIN A	2%
CARBOHYDRATE	14 g	VITAMIN C	*
FAT	6 g	THIAMINE	2%
CHOLESTEROL	10 mg	RIBOFLAVIN	2%
SODIUM	50 mg	NIACIN	*
POTASSIUM	70 mg	CALCIUM	2%
		IRON	2%

* Contains less than 2% of the U.S. RDA of this nutrient.

This yummy cookie pizza is perfect to serve for special occasions. For easier serving, use a sharp, wet knife to cut the pizza into small wedges or squares.

ROCKY ROAD COOKIE PIZZA

(pictured on left)

**1 (20-oz.) pkg. Pillsbury's BEST®
Refrigerated Sugar Cookies**
½ cup chopped salted peanuts
1 cup miniature marshmallows
**1 (6-oz.) pkg. (1 cup) semi-
sweet chocolate chips**
**⅓ cup caramel ice cream
topping**

Heat oven to 350°F. Line 12-inch pizza pan with foil; grease foil. Press cookie dough into bottom of foil-lined pan.

Bake at 350°F. for 13 to 16 minutes or until light golden brown. Remove from oven. Sprinkle evenly with peanuts, marshmallows and chocolate chips. Drizzle with caramel topping. Bake an additional 5 to 10 minutes or until golden brown. Cool completely. Remove foil from cookie pizza. Cut into wedges or squares. 16 servings.

NUTRITION INFORMATION

SERVING SIZE: 1/16 OF RECIPE		PERCENT U.S. RDA PER SERVING	
CALORIES	260	PROTEIN	6%
PROTEIN	4 g	VITAMIN A	*
CARBOHYDRATE	36 g	VITAMIN C	*
FAT	12 g	THIAMINE	4%
CHOLESTEROL	4 mg	RIBOFLAVIN	4%
SODIUM	200 mg	NIACIN	8%
POTASSIUM	90 mg	CALCIUM	*
		IRON	6%

* Contains less than 2% of the U.S. RDA of this nutrient.

These tiny little morsels are just right for a special party tray. For the smoothest meringue, be sure to add the sugar about one tablespoon at a time so that it completely dissolves during the beating.

PEPPERMINT MERINGUE BITES

(pictured on p. 21)

2 egg whites
¼ teaspoon cream of tartar
¼ teaspoon peppermint extract
⅔ cup sugar
**1 tablespoon finely crushed
hard peppermint candy**

Heat oven to 250°F. Line cookie sheets with foil. In small bowl, beat egg whites, cream of tartar and peppermint extract until foamy. Gradually add sugar 1 tablespoon at a time, beating 3 to 5 minutes or until stiff peaks form. Pipe or spoon 1¼-inch mounds on foil-lined cookie sheets. Sprinkle each lightly with peppermint candy.

Bake at 250°F. for 25 to 35 minutes or until crisp and dry. Cool completely; remove from cookie sheets.
3 dozen cookies.

NUTRITION INFORMATION

SERVING SIZE: 1 COOKIE		PERCENT U.S. RDA PER SERVING	
CALORIES	16	PROTEIN	*
PROTEIN	0 g	VITAMIN A	*
CARBOHYDRATE	4 g	VITAMIN C	*
FAT	0 g	THIAMINE	*
CHOLESTEROL	0 mg	RIBOFLAVIN	*
SODIUM	0 mg	NIACIN	*
POTASSIUM	0 mg	CALCIUM	*
		IRON	*

* Contains less than 2% of the U.S. RDA of this nutrient.

Rocky Road Cookie Pizza

There is no substitute for real brandy in these elegant dessert cookies. Plan to serve them for an extra special occasion.

Macaroons are typically made from egg whites, sugar, and almonds or coconut. This version adds pineapple for a fruit-flavored, chewy cookie.

BRANDY CREAM-FILLED COOKIES

(pictured on right)

1 (3-oz.) pkg. cream cheese, softened
¼ cup powdered sugar
2 tablespoons brandy
½ cup whipping cream, whipped
2 (5½-oz.) pkg. pirouette or tubular-shaped cookies
⅓ cup semi-sweet chocolate chips
½ teaspoon shortening

In medium bowl, beat cream cheese, powdered sugar and brandy until fluffy. Fold in whipped cream.* Using decorating bag fitted with ¼-inch tip or resealable plastic bag with a small cut in one corner, carefully pipe mixture into cookies.

In small saucepan over low heat, melt chocolate chips and shortening, stirring constantly. Drizzle over cookies. Serve immediately or refrigerate up to 2 hours. Store in refrigerator. 4 dozen cookies.

TIP:
* Cream cheese mixture can be made up to 4 hours in advance. Refrigerate filling until ready to use.

NUTRITION INFORMATION

SERVING SIZE: 1 COOKIE		PERCENT U.S. RDA PER SERVING	
CALORIES	60	PROTEIN	*
PROTEIN	0 g	VITAMIN A	*
CARBOHYDRATE	6 g	VITAMIN C	*
FAT	4 g	THIAMINE	*
CHOLESTEROL	8 mg	RIBOFLAVIN	*
SODIUM	25 mg	NIACIN	*
POTASSIUM	10 mg	CALCIUM	*
		IRON	*

* Contains less than 2% of the U.S. RDA of this nutrient.

PINEAPPLE MACAROONS

(pictured on right)

4 egg whites
⅔ cup sugar
½ cup Pillsbury's BEST® All Purpose or Unbleached Flour
⅛ teaspoon salt
1 (8-oz.) can crushed pineapple, well drained
4 cups coconut

Heat oven to 325°F. Line 2 cookie sheets with parchment paper or grease and lightly flour. In large bowl, beat egg whites until foamy. Gradually add sugar 1 tablespoon at a time, beating until stiff peaks form. Lightly spoon flour into measuring cup; level off. Fold in flour and salt. Stir in pineapple and coconut. Drop dough by tablespoonfuls 2 inches apart onto parchment-lined cookie sheets.

Bake at 325°F. for 12 to 17 minutes or until set and lightly browned. Cool 1 minute; remove from cookie sheets. Cool completely. 24 cookies.

NUTRITION INFORMATION

SERVING SIZE: 1 COOKIE		PERCENT U.S. RDA PER SERVING	
CALORIES	100	PROTEIN	2%
PROTEIN	1 g	VITAMIN A	*
CARBOHYDRATE	14 g	VITAMIN C	*
FAT	4 g	THIAMINE	2%
CHOLESTEROL	0 mg	RIBOFLAVIN	2%
SODIUM	25 mg	NIACIN	*
POTASSIUM	65 mg	CALCIUM	*
		IRON	2%

* Contains less than 2% of the U.S. RDA of this nutrient.

Pineapple Macaroons,
Brandy Cream-Filled Cookies,
Peppermint Meringue Bites p. 19

Carob chips are available in health food, specialty and some large grocery stores. Carob comes from a tropical tree and starts as a sweet, edible pulp. The pulp is dried and then used for making baking products. Carob has a subtle chocolate-like flavor and texture.

CAROB CHIP OATMEAL COOKIES

¾ cup firmly packed brown
    sugar
¾ cup sugar
½ cup margarine or butter,
    softened
½ cup shortening
1 teaspoon vanilla
2 eggs
1 cup Pillsbury's BEST® All
    Purpose or Unbleached
    Flour
½ cup Pillsbury's BEST® Whole
    Wheat Flour
1 teaspoon baking soda
1 teaspoon salt
2 cups quick-cooking rolled
    oats
1 (6-oz.) pkg. (1 cup) carob
    chips or semi-sweet
    chocolate chips
½ cup chopped nuts or unsalted
    shelled sunflower seeds, if
    desired

Heat oven to 350°F. Grease cookie sheets. In large bowl, beat brown sugar, sugar, margarine and shortening until light and fluffy. Add vanilla and eggs; blend well. Lightly spoon flour into measuring cup; level off. Stir in all purpose flour, whole wheat flour, baking soda and salt; mix well. Stir in oats, carob chips and nuts. Drop dough by rounded teaspoonfuls 2 inches apart onto greased cookie sheets.

Bake at 350°F. for 10 to 15 minutes or until light golden brown. Cool 1 minute; remove from cookie sheets. 6 dozen cookies.

HIGH ALTITUDE – Above 3500 Feet: Increase all purpose flour to 1 cup plus 3 tablespoons. Bake as directed above.

NUTRITION INFORMATION

SERVING SIZE: 1 COOKIE		PERCENT U.S. RDA PER SERVING	
CALORIES	70	PROTEIN	*
PROTEIN	1 g	VITAMIN A	*
CARBOHYDRATE	9 g	VITAMIN C	*
FAT	4 g	THIAMINE	2%
CHOLESTEROL	6 mg	RIBOFLAVIN	*
SODIUM	65 mg	NIACIN	*
POTASSIUM	30 mg	CALCIUM	*
		IRON	*

* Contains less than 2% of the U.S. RDA of this nutrient.

This thick, chewy oatmeal cookie can be made with quick-cooking or old-fashioned rolled oats. Cookies made with old-fashioned rolled oats have a moister, coarser texture. If the candy-coated chips are not available, chocolate chips are a good substitute.

NUTRITION INFORMATION

SERVING SIZE:
1 COOKIE

		PERCENT U.S. RDA PER SERVING	
CALORIES	130	PROTEIN	2%
PROTEIN	2 g	VITAMIN A	2%
CARBOHYDRATE	18 g	VITAMIN C	*
FAT	6 g	THIAMINE	4%
CHOLESTEROL	9 mg	RIBOFLAVIN	2%
SODIUM	110 mg	NIACIN	*
POTASSIUM	50 mg	CALCIUM	2%
		IRON	4%

* Contains less than 2% of the U.S. RDA of this nutrient.

OATMEAL COCONUT FUN CHIPPERS

1½ cups firmly packed brown sugar
 1 cup margarine or butter, softened
 1 tablespoon milk
 1 tablespoon vanilla
 2 eggs
2¼ cups Pillsbury's BEST® All Purpose or Unbleached Flour
 2 teaspoons baking powder
 1 teaspoon baking soda
 ½ teaspoon salt
 2 cups rolled oats
 1 cup coconut
 1 (10-oz.) pkg. multi-colored candy-coated chocolate chips or 1½ cups semi-sweet chocolate chips

Heat oven to 375°F. In large bowl, beat brown sugar and margarine until light and fluffy. Add milk, vanilla and eggs; blend well. Lightly spoon flour into measuring cup; level off. Stir in flour, baking powder, baking soda and salt; mix well. Stir in oats, coconut and chocolate chips. Drop dough by rounded tablespoonfuls 2 inches apart onto ungreased cookie sheets.

Bake at 375°F. for 9 to 13 minutes or until light golden brown. Cool 1 minute; remove from cookie sheets. Cool completely. 4 dozen cookies.

HIGH ALTITUDE – Above 3500 Feet: Decrease brown sugar to 1¼ cups. Increase flour to 2½ cups. Bake as directed above.

Cook's Note

ROLLED OATS

Rolled oats can be purchased in three varieties: old-fashioned, quick-cooking and instant. **Old-fashioned** rolled oats are whole oats that have been hulled, steamed and flattened by rollers into flakes. **Quick-cooking** rolled oats have been cut into smaller pieces before rolling, yielding thinner flakes that cook more quickly. **Instant oats** have been cut into even smaller pieces, precooked and dried so that they cook very fast.

Old-fashioned and quick-cooking rolled oats can usually be used interchangeably in our recipes unless we specify a variety. However, old-fashioned rolled oats will result in a firmer textured end product. Instant oats are not usually used for baking; most instant oat products include sugar, salt or flavorings and are meant to be used primarily as breakfast cereal.

These easy cookies from the fourth Pillsbury BAKE-OFF® Contest have become a classic favorite.

CHOCOLATE PIXIES

(pictured on right and cover)

¼ cup margarine or butter
4 oz. (4 squares) unsweetened
   chocolate
2 cups Pillsbury's BEST® All
   Purpose or Unbleached
   Flour
2 cups sugar
½ cup chopped walnuts or
   pecans
2 teaspoons baking powder
½ teaspoon salt
4 eggs
   Powdered sugar

In large saucepan over low heat, melt margarine and chocolate, stirring constantly until smooth. Remove from heat; cool slightly. Lightly spoon flour into measuring cup; level off. Stir in flour, sugar, walnuts, baking powder, salt and eggs; mix well. Cover with plastic wrap; refrigerate at least 1 hour for easier handling.

Heat oven to 300°F. Shape dough into 1-inch balls; roll each in powdered sugar, coating heavily. Place 2 inches apart on ungreased cookie sheets. Bake at 300°F. for 13 to 18 minutes or until set. Immediately remove from cookie sheets. Cool completely.
4 dozen cookies.

HIGH ALTITUDE – Above 3500 Feet: Increase flour to 2¼ cups. Bake as directed above.

NUTRITION INFORMATION

SERVING SIZE: 1 COOKIE		PERCENT U.S. RDA PER SERVING	
CALORIES	80	PROTEIN	2%
PROTEIN	1 g	VITAMIN A	*
CARBOHYDRATE	12 g	VITAMIN C	*
FAT	3 g	THIAMINE	2%
CHOLESTEROL	18 mg	RIBOFLAVIN	2%
SODIUM	50 mg	NIACIN	*
POTASSIUM	35 mg	CALCIUM	*
		IRON	2%

* Contains less than 2% of the U.S. RDA of this nutrient.

Chocolate Pixies

We've created an incredibly delicious recipe for chocolate chip cookies. Baking them just until light golden brown ensures chewy, moist cookies. If you like them crisper, bake them one to two minutes longer.

NUTRITION INFORMATION

SERVING SIZE: 1 COOKIE		PERCENT U.S. RDA PER SERVING	
CALORIES	180	PROTEIN	2%
PROTEIN	2 g	VITAMIN A	4%
CARBOHYDRATE	21 g	VITAMIN C	*
FAT	10 g	THIAMINE	6%
CHOLESTEROL	10 mg	RIBOFLAVIN	4%
SODIUM	115 mg	NIACIN	2%
POTASSIUM	80 mg	CALCIUM	2%
		IRON	4%

* Contains less than 2% of the U.S. RDA of this nutrient.

CHOCOLATE CHIP COOKIES SUPREME

1 cup sugar
1 cup firmly packed brown sugar
1½ cups margarine or butter, softened
2 teaspoons vanilla
½ teaspoon rum extract
2 eggs
3 cups Pillsbury's BEST® All Purpose or Unbleached Flour
1½ cups oat bran
1 teaspoon baking powder
1 teaspoon baking soda
¼ teaspoon salt
1 (6-oz.) pkg. (1 cup) semi-sweet chocolate chips
1 (6-oz.) white baking bar, chopped, or 1 cup vanilla milk chips
1 cup chopped walnuts or pecans

Heat oven to 375°F. In large bowl, beat sugar, brown sugar and margarine until light and fluffy. Add vanilla, rum extract and eggs; blend well. Lightly spoon flour into measuring cup; level off. Stir in flour, oat bran, baking powder, baking soda and salt; mix well. Stir in chocolate chips, white baking bar and walnuts. (Dough will be stiff.) Drop dough by rounded tablespoonfuls 2 inches apart onto ungreased cookie sheets.

Bake at 375°F. for 9 to 15 minutes or until light golden brown. Cool 1 minute; remove from cookie sheets. 4 dozen cookies.

HIGH ALTITUDE – Above 3500 Feet: Decrease white sugar to ½ cup. Increase flour to 3½ cups. Bake as directed above.

This chocolate cookie dough is shaped easily into playful little creatures. Store these cookies in a single layer tightly covered and serve them anytime a little whimsy is needed!

CHOCOLATE COOKIE MICE

(pictured on p. 48)

¾ cup sugar
½ cup margarine or butter, softened
½ cup shortening
1 teaspoon vanilla
1 egg
2¼ cups Pillsbury's BEST® All Purpose or Unbleached Flour
¼ cup unsweetened cocoa
½ teaspoon baking powder
Miniature semi-sweet chocolate chips
Red or black string licorice, cut into 2-inch pieces

Heat oven to 325°F. In large bowl, beat sugar, margarine and shortening until light and fluffy. Add vanilla and egg; blend well. Lightly spoon flour into measuring cup; level off. Stir in flour, cocoa and baking powder; mix well. Shape dough into 1-inch balls.

To form mouse, pinch one end of ball to form nose. For ears, make two tiny balls of dough and flatten slightly; gently press into dough on upper front of each mouse body. For eyes, press 2 miniature chocolate chips into dough below ears. Place shaped cookies 2 inches apart on ungreased cookie sheets.

Bake at 325°F. for 8 to 13 minutes or until set. For mouse tails, immediately place piece of licorice into rounded end of each cookie. Remove from cookie sheets. 3 dozen cookies.

HIGH ALTITUDE – Above 3500 Feet: Increase flour to 2½ cups. Bake as directed above.

NUTRITION INFORMATION

SERVING SIZE: 1 COOKIE		PERCENT U.S. RDA PER SERVING	
CALORIES	100	PROTEIN	*
PROTEIN	1 g	VITAMIN A	2%
CARBOHYDRATE	11 g	VITAMIN C	*
FAT	6 g	THIAMINE	4%
CHOLESTEROL	6 mg	RIBOFLAVIN	2%
SODIUM	40 mg	NIACIN	2%
POTASSIUM	15 mg	CALCIUM	*
		IRON	2%

* Contains less than 2% of the U.S. RDA of this nutrient.

VARIATION: CHOCOLATY SHORTBREAD COOKIES: Prepare cookie dough as directed above. Shape dough into 1-inch balls. Place 2 inches apart on ungreased cookie sheets. Flatten slightly with glass dipped in sugar. Bake at 325°F. for 8 to 13 minutes or until set. Cool 1 minute; remove from cookie sheets.

Pillsbury Refrigerated Pie Crusts make it so easy to create elegant little pastry cookies.

CHOCOLATE PECAN TASSIES

1 (15-oz.) pkg. Pillsbury All Ready Pie Crusts
2 teaspoons flour

FILLING
⅔ cup chopped pecans
¾ cup firmly packed brown sugar
1 tablespoon margarine or butter, softened
1 teaspoon vanilla
1 oz. (1 square) semi-sweet chocolate, melted, cooled
1 egg

Allow both crust pouches to stand at room temperature for 15 to 20 minutes. Heat oven to 375°F.

Unfold each crust; remove top plastic sheets. Press out fold lines. Sprinkle each with 1 teaspoon flour. Spread flour evenly over crusts. Invert and remove remaining plastic sheets. Using a 2⅝ to 2¾-inch round, scalloped cookie cutter, cut 12 rounds out of each crust. Gently press rounds, floured side down, into 24 ungreased miniature muffin cups.

Sprinkle ⅓ cup of the pecans evenly into pie crust-lined muffin cups. In small bowl, beat brown sugar, margarine, vanilla, chocolate and egg just until smooth (do not overbeat; mixture should not be bubbly). Spoon teaspoonful of filling over pecans in each cup. Sprinkle with remaining ⅓ cup pecans.

Bake at 375°F. for 18 to 22 minutes or until filling is set and crust is light golden brown. Cool 1 minute; remove from pans. 24 cookies.

NUTRITION INFORMATION

SERVING SIZE: 1 COOKIE		PERCENT U.S. RDA PER SERVING	
CALORIES	140	PROTEIN	*
PROTEIN	1 g	VITAMIN A	*
CARBOHYDRATE	16 g	VITAMIN C	*
FAT	8 g	THIAMINE	*
CHOLESTEROL	13 mg	RIBOFLAVIN	*
SODIUM	75 mg	NIACIN	*
POTASSIUM	55 mg	CALCIUM	*
		IRON	2%

* Contains less than 2% of the U.S. RDA of this nutrient.

To make the frosting faces, use a small plastic decorator bottle filled with frosting and fitted with a writing tip. Or, place the frosting in a resealable plastic bag and make a very small cut in one corner. Squeeze the frosting gently through the opening.

CHOCOLATE RAISIN SMILE COOKIES

COOKIES

1½ cups sugar
 1 cup firmly packed brown
    sugar
1½ cups margarine or butter,
    softened
 2 teaspoons vanilla
 3 eggs
 3 cups Pillsbury's BEST® All
    Purpose or Unbleached
    Flour
 1 cup unsweetened cocoa
 1 teaspoon baking soda
 ¼ teaspoon salt
 2 cups raisins

FROSTING

 1 cup powdered sugar
 1 drop red food color
 2 drops yellow food color
 2 to 4 teaspoons milk

Heat oven to 350°F. In large bowl, beat sugar, brown sugar and margarine until light and fluffy. Add vanilla and eggs; blend well. Lightly spoon flour into measuring cup; level off. Stir in flour, cocoa, baking soda and salt; mix well. Stir in raisins. Drop dough by rounded tablespoonfuls 2 inches apart onto ungreased cookie sheets.

Bake at 350°F. for 10 to 14 minutes or until slightly set. Cool 1 minute; remove from cookie sheets.

In medium bowl, combine all frosting ingredients, adding enough milk for desired decorating consistency. Using decorating bag, decorating bottle, plastic bag or small spoon , make smiling faces on cookies.
5 dozen cookies.

HIGH ALTITUDE – Above 3500 Feet: Decrease sugar to 1¼ cups. Decrease brown sugar to ¾ cup. Increase flour to 3½ cups. Bake as directed above.

NUTRITION INFORMATION

SERVING SIZE: 1 COOKIE		PERCENT U.S. RDA PER SERVING	
CALORIES	130	PROTEIN	2%
PROTEIN	1 g	VITAMIN A	4%
CARBOHYDRATE	20 g	VITAMIN C	*
FAT	5 g	THIAMINE	4%
CHOLESTEROL	11 mg	RIBOFLAVIN	2%
SODIUM	95 mg	NIACIN	2%
POTASSIUM	70 mg	CALCIUM	*
		IRON	4%

* Contains less than 2% of the U.S. RDA of this nutrient.

VARIATION: (Pictured on left) GIANT SMILE COOKIES: Prepare cookie dough as directed above. For each cookie, place ¼ cup of the dough 3 inches apart on ungreased cookie sheets. Bake at 350°F. for 10 to 14 minutes or until slightly set. Continue as directed above.
2½ dozen cookies.

Cook's Note

RAISINS

Raisins add natural sweetness to baked products and are great as a wholesome snack.

Raisins are grapes that are harvested and sun-dried for three to five weeks. An exception to this is golden raisins, known for their amber color and moist texture. They are not sun-dried and are sent for processing immediately after harvest. Golden raisins are dipped in hot water and treated with sulfur dioxide to retain color, then dried in dehydrators.

Most raisins come from Thompson Seedless grapes, but Muscat and Sultana varieties are also used. Most raisins are grown in California.

Store raisins tightly covered in a cool, dry place. They will keep well for up to six months.

After the frosting has set up, store these cookies between layers of waxed paper in a tightly covered container.

ORANGE CAPPUCCINO DROPS

COOKIES
- 1 cup firmly packed brown sugar
- ½ cup margarine or butter, softened
- ⅔ cup dairy sour cream
- ½ cup strong coffee*
- 3 oz. (3 squares) unsweetened chocolate, melted, cooled
- 1 egg
- 1 teaspoon vanilla
- 2 cups Pillsbury's BEST® All Purpose or Unbleached Flour
- ½ teaspoon baking soda

FROSTING
- 2 cups powdered sugar
- 2 tablespoons margarine or butter, melted
- 1½ teaspoons grated orange peel
- 2 to 3 tablespoons milk

Heat oven to 375°F. In large bowl, beat brown sugar and ½ cup margarine until light and fluffy. Add sour cream, coffee, chocolate, egg and vanilla; blend well. Lightly spoon flour into measuring cup; level off. Stir in flour and baking soda; mix well. (Cookie dough will be very soft.) Drop dough by teaspoonfuls 2 inches apart onto ungreased cookie sheets.

Bake at 375°F. for 5 to 7 minutes or until set. Immediately remove from cookie sheets. Cool completely.

In small bowl, combine all frosting ingredients, adding enough milk for desired spreading consistency. Frost cooled cookies. Let stand until set. 5 dozen cookies.

TIP:
* Two teaspoons instant coffee dissolved in ½ cup hot water can be substituted for strong coffee.

HIGH ALTITUDE – Above 3500 Feet: No change.

NUTRITION INFORMATION

SERVING SIZE: 1 COOKIE		PERCENT U.S. RDA PER SERVING	
CALORIES	80	PROTEIN	*
PROTEIN	1 g	VITAMIN A	2%
CARBOHYDRATE	12 g	VITAMIN C	*
FAT	3 g	THIAMINE	2%
CHOLESTEROL	5 mg	RIBOFLAVIN	*
SODIUM	35 mg	NIACIN	*
POTASSIUM	35 mg	CALCIUM	*
		IRON	2%

* Contains less than 2% of the U.S. RDA of this nutrient.

These tender drop cookies are chock full of carrots, walnuts and raisins. They're topped with a quick and easy frosting.

FROSTED CARROT DROPS

COOKIES
- ¾ cup sugar
- 1 cup margarine or butter, softened
- 1 teaspoon vanilla
- 1 egg
- 2 cups Pillsbury's BEST® All Purpose or Unbleached Flour
- 1 teaspoon baking powder
- ½ teaspoon salt
- 1 cup finely shredded carrots
- ½ cup chopped walnuts or pecans
- ½ cup raisins

FROSTING
- 1 can Pillsbury Vanilla Frosting Supreme™
- 1 tablespoon grated orange peel

Heat oven to 350°F. In large bowl, beat sugar and margarine until light and fluffy. Add vanilla and egg; blend well. Lightly spoon flour into measuring cup; level off. Stir in flour, baking powder and salt; mix well. Stir in carrots, walnuts and raisins. Drop dough by teaspoonfuls 2 inches apart onto ungreased cookie sheets.

Bake at 350°F. for 8 to 12 minutes or until edges are light golden brown. Remove from cookie sheets; cool completely.

In small bowl, combine frosting and orange peel; mix well. Frost cooled cookies. 4½ dozen cookies.

HIGH ALTITUDE – Above 3500 Feet: No change.

NUTRITION INFORMATION

SERVING SIZE: 1 COOKIE		PERCENT U.S. RDA PER SERVING	
CALORIES	110	PROTEIN	*
PROTEIN	1 g	VITAMIN A	15%
CARBOHYDRATE	14 g	VITAMIN C	*
FAT	6 g	THIAMINE	2%
CHOLESTEROL	4 mg	RIBOFLAVIN	*
SODIUM	80 mg	NIACIN	*
POTASSIUM	35 mg	CALCIUM	*
		IRON	*

* Contains less than 2% of the U.S. RDA of this nutrient.

Black-eyed Susans are yellow daisy-like flowers that bloom in profusion in the early fall. Our cookie version is tender and delicate with just a hint of lemon.

LEMON BLACK-EYED SUSAN COOKIES

1 cup sugar
1 cup margarine or butter, softened
3 tablespoons lemon juice
1 egg
3 cups Pillsbury's BEST® All Purpose or Unbleached Flour
1½ teaspoons baking powder
¼ teaspoon salt
1 egg yolk
1 teaspoon water
Few drops yellow food color
¾ cup semi-sweet chocolate chips

In large bowl, beat sugar and margarine until light and fluffy. Add lemon juice and egg; blend well. Lightly spoon flour into measuring cup; level off. Stir in flour, baking powder and salt; mix well. Cover with plastic wrap; refrigerate 1 hour for easier handling.

Heat oven to 400°F. On lightly floured surface, roll half of dough to ¼-inch thickness. Cut with floured 2 to 3-inch flower-shaped cookie cutter. Place 1 inch apart on ungreased cookie sheets. Repeat with second half of dough. In small bowl, combine egg yolk and water; blend well. Stir in food color. Brush tops of cookies with egg yolk mixture.

Bake at 400°F. for 5 to 7 minutes or until edges are light golden brown. Immediately place chocolate chip in center of each cookie. Remove from cookie sheets. 5½ dozen cookies.

HIGH ALTITUDE – Above 3500 Feet: No change.

NUTRITION INFORMATION

SERVING SIZE: 1 COOKIE		PERCENT U.S. RDA PER SERVING	
CALORIES	70	PROTEIN	*
PROTEIN	1 g	VITAMIN A	2%
CARBOHYDRATE	9 g	VITAMIN C	*
FAT	4 g	THIAMINE	2%
CHOLESTEROL	7 mg	RIBOFLAVIN	2%
SODIUM	50 mg	NIACIN	*
POTASSIUM	15 mg	CALCIUM	*
		IRON	*

* Contains less than 2% of the U.S. RDA of this nutrient.

To save time and add color, shred unpeeled zucchini in the food processor. Store these soft-textured cookies between sheets of waxed paper in a tightly covered container.

These chewy, chocolaty brownie cookies are deliciously minty. Store them between sheets of waxed paper in a tightly covered container.

CHOCOLATE ZUCCHINI DROPS

(pictured on right)

- **1 pkg. Pillsbury Plus® Devil's Food Cake Mix**
- **1 cup rolled oats**
- **1 cup shredded zucchini**
- **½ cup margarine or butter, melted**
- **2 eggs**
- **½ cup chopped walnuts or pecans**

Heat oven to 350°F. Lightly grease cookie sheets. In large bowl, combine all ingredients except walnuts; mix well. Stir in walnuts. Drop dough by rounded teaspoonfuls 2 inches apart onto greased cookie sheets.

Bake at 350°F. for 8 to 11 minutes or until set. Cool 1 minute; remove from cookie sheets. 4 dozen cookies.

HIGH ALTITUDE – Above 3500 Feet: Add 2 tablespoons flour to dry cake mix. Bake as directed above.

NUTRITION INFORMATION

SERVING SIZE: 1 COOKIE		PERCENT U.S. RDA PER SERVING	
CALORIES	80	PROTEIN	*
PROTEIN	1 g	VITAMIN A	2%
CARBOHYDRATE	10 g	VITAMIN C	*
FAT	4 g	THIAMINE	2%
CHOLESTEROL	9 mg	RIBOFLAVIN	*
SODIUM	105 mg	NIACIN	*
POTASSIUM	65 mg	CALCIUM	2%
		IRON	*

* Contains less than 2% of the U.S. RDA of this nutrient.

MINT CHIP BROWNIE COOKIES

(pictured on right)

COOKIES
- **1 (21½-oz.) pkg. Pillsbury Fudge Brownie Mix**
- **⅓ cup oil**
- **2 eggs**
- **1 (10-oz.) pkg. (1½ cups) mint-flavored chocolate chips, reserving ½ cup for glaze**
- **¼ cup chopped nuts**

GLAZE
- **Reserved ½ cup mint-flavored chocolate chips**
- **2 tablespoons margarine or butter**

Heat oven to 350°F. In large bowl, combine brownie mix, oil and eggs. By hand, stir with spoon until well blended. Stir in 1 cup mint-flavored chips and nuts. Drop dough by rounded teaspoonfuls 2 inches apart onto ungreased cookie sheets.

Bake at 350°F. for 9 to 13 minutes or until set. Cool 1 minute; remove from cookie sheets.

In small saucepan over low heat, melt chocolate chips and margarine, stirring constantly. Drizzle over cookies. Let stand until set. 4 dozen cookies.

HIGH ALTITUDE – Above 3500 Feet: Add ¼ cup flour to dry brownie mix. Bake as directed above.

NUTRITION INFORMATION

SERVING SIZE: 1 COOKIE		PERCENT U.S. RDA PER SERVING	
CALORIES	110	PROTEIN	*
PROTEIN	1 g	VITAMIN A	*
CARBOHYDRATE	14 g	VITAMIN C	*
FAT	6 g	THIAMINE	*
CHOLESTEROL	9 mg	RIBOFLAVIN	*
SODIUM	50 mg	NIACIN	*
POTASSIUM	50 mg	CALCIUM	*
		IRON	2%

* Contains less than 2% of the U.S. RDA of this nutrient.

Chocolate Zucchini Drops,
Mint Chip Brownie Cookies

EASY GRASSHOPPER SANDWICH COOKIES

¼ cup butter or margarine, softened
2 tablespoons shortening
1¼ cups powdered sugar
⅛ teaspoon salt
2 tablespoons creme de menthe liqueur
1 (8½-oz.) pkg. chocolate wafer cookies

In small bowl, beat butter and shortening until combined. Add powdered sugar, salt and liqueur; beat until light and fluffy. Spread scant tablespoonful powdered sugar mixture on wafer cookie; top with another wafer cookie, pressing lightly. Repeat with remaining cookies and powdered sugar mixture. Refrigerate until set.
20 sandwich cookies.

TIP:
    A few additional drops of creme de menthe can be added to filling mixture if it becomes too stiff to spread.

NUTRITION INFORMATION

SERVING SIZE: 1 COOKIE		PERCENT U.S. RDA PER SERVING	
CALORIES	120	PROTEIN	*
PROTEIN	1 g	VITAMIN A	2%
CARBOHYDRATE	17 g	VITAMIN C	*
FAT	5 g	THIAMINE	2%
CHOLESTEROL	11 mg	RIBOFLAVIN	*
SODIUM	55 mg	NIACIN	*
POTASSIUM	15 mg	CALCIUM	*
		IRON	2%

* Contains less than 2% of the U.S. RDA of this nutrient.

TOFFEE CRISPS

1 cup sugar
½ cup firmly packed brown sugar
½ cup margarine or butter, softened
1 teaspoon vanilla
2 eggs
2¼ cups Pillsbury's BEST® All Purpose or Unbleached Flour
1 teaspoon baking powder
½ teaspoon baking soda
½ teaspoon salt
1 (6-oz.) pkg. almond brickle baking chips

Heat oven to 375°F. Grease cookie sheets. In large bowl, beat sugar, brown sugar and margarine until light and fluffy. Add vanilla and eggs; blend well. Lightly spoon flour into measuring cup; level off. Stir in flour, baking powder, baking soda and salt; mix well. Stir in baking chips. Drop dough by rounded teaspoonfuls 2 inches apart onto greased cookie sheets.

Bake at 375°F. for 8 to 12 minutes or until light golden brown. Immediately remove from cookie sheets. Cool completely. 5 to 6 dozen cookies.

HIGH ALTITUDE – Above 3500 Feet: No change.

NUTRITION INFORMATION

SERVING SIZE: 1 COOKIE		PERCENT U.S. RDA PER SERVING	
CALORIES	60	PROTEIN	*
PROTEIN	1 g	VITAMIN A	*
CARBOHYDRATE	9 g	VITAMIN C	*
FAT	2 g	THIAMINE	2%
CHOLESTEROL	6 mg	RIBOFLAVIN	*
SODIUM	45 mg	NIACIN	*
POTASSIUM	10 mg	CALCIUM	*
		IRON	*

* Contains less than 2% of the U.S. RDA of this nutrient.

There are few ingredients in this buttery, melt-in-your-mouth shortbread. For a change of pace, follow our easy directions to make triangular bars.

CHOCOLATE SHORTBREAD

1 cup powdered sugar
1 cup butter or margarine, softened
1 teaspoon vanilla
2 cups Pillsbury's BEST® All Purpose or Unbleached Flour
¼ cup unsweetened cocoa

Heat oven to 325°F. In large bowl, beat powdered sugar and butter until light and fluffy. Add vanilla; blend well. Lightly spoon flour into measuring cup; level off. Stir in flour and cocoa; mix well. On ungreased cookie sheet, press dough out to form 12x6-inch rectangle, about ½ inch thick. Prick thoroughly with fork.

Bake at 325°F. for 20 minutes or until slightly firm to touch. Immediately cut into bars.* Cool 5 minutes; remove from cookie sheet. Cool completely on wire rack. 32 cookies.

TIP:
* To make triangular bars, cut dough crosswise into four 3-inch strips. Cut in half lengthwise forming eight 3x3-inch squares. Divide each square into 4 triangles by cutting diagonally from corner to corner.

HIGH ALTITUDE – Above 3500 Feet: No change.

NUTRITION INFORMATION

SERVING SIZE: 1 COOKIE		PERCENT U.S. RDA PER SERVING	
CALORIES	100	PROTEIN	*
PROTEIN	1 g	VITAMIN A	4%
CARBOHYDRATE	10 g	VITAMIN C	*
FAT	6 g	THIAMINE	4%
CHOLESTEROL	16 mg	RIBOFLAVIN	2%
SODIUM	65 mg	NIACIN	2%
POTASSIUM	15 mg	CALCIUM	*
		IRON	2%

* Contains less than 2% of the U.S. RDA of this nutrient.

A rich and flavorful drop cookie.

DATE NUT MACAROONS

⅔ cup Pillsbury's BEST® All Purpose or Unbleached Flour
1 (14-oz.) pkg. (5⅓ cups) coconut
¼ teaspoon salt
1 (14-oz.) can sweetened condensed milk (not evaporated)
1 cup chopped dates
1 cup chopped walnuts

Heat oven to 350°F. Grease cookie sheets. Lightly spoon flour into measuring cup; level off. In large bowl, combine flour, coconut and salt; mix well. Stir in milk. Fold in dates and walnuts. Drop by tablespoons onto greased cookie sheets. Bake at 350°F. for 12 to 15 minutes or until light golden brown. 4½ dozen cookies.

HIGH ALTITUDE – Above 3500 Feet: No change.

NUTRITION INFORMATION

SERVING SIZE: 1 COOKIE		PERCENT U.S. RDA PER SERVING	
CALORIES	90	PROTEIN	2%
PROTEIN	1 g	VITAMIN A	*
CARBOHYDRATE	12 g	VITAMIN C	*
FAT	4 g	THIAMINE	2%
CHOLESTEROL	2 mg	RIBOFLAVIN	2%
SODIUM	20 mg	NIACIN	*
POTASSIUM	85 mg	CALCIUM	2%
		IRON	*

* Contains less than 2% of the U.S. RDA of this nutrient.

These candy-filled cookies won rave reviews from our taste panel of home economists. The flavor combination is delectable, and refrigerated cookie dough makes them easy to prepare.

GIANT PEANUT BUTTER ZEBRA COOKIES

(pictured on right)

1 (20-oz.) pkg. Pillsbury's BEST® Refrigerated Peanut Butter Cookies
12 miniature peanut butter cup candies, unwrapped
⅓ cup semi-sweet chocolate chips
1 teaspoon shortening

Heat oven to 350°F. Divide cookie dough into 12 equal pieces. Wrap 1 piece of dough around each peanut butter cup, shaping into a ball. Place 6 balls on ungreased cookie sheet, spaced evenly apart. Refrigerate remaining 6 balls until ready to bake.

Bake at 350°F. for 11 to 15 minutes or until golden brown. Cool 1 minute; remove from cookie sheet. Cool completely. Repeat with remaining 6 balls.

In small saucepan over low heat, melt chocolate chips and shortening, stirring constantly. Drizzle over cooled cookies in crisscross pattern. Let stand until glaze is set. 12 cookies.

NUTRITION INFORMATION

SERVING SIZE: 1 COOKIE		PERCENT U.S. RDA PER SERVING	
CALORIES	260	PROTEIN	6%
PROTEIN	4 g	VITAMIN A	*
CARBOHYDRATE	32 g	VITAMIN C	*
FAT	13 g	THIAMINE	4%
CHOLESTEROL	11 mg	RIBOFLAVIN	8%
SODIUM	250 mg	NIACIN	8%
POTASSIUM	105 mg	CALCIUM	*
		IRON	4%

* Contains less than 2% of the U.S. RDA of this nutrient.

Giant Peanut Butter Zebra Cookies

To preserve their freshness, store these lemony morsels tightly covered. They are more tender when made with butter, but regular margarine is an acceptable alternative.

⬥

LEMON BUTTER COOKIES

½ cup sugar
½ cup powdered sugar
¾ cup butter or margarine, softened
¼ cup oil
1 tablespoon grated lemon peel
1 tablespoon lemon juice
1 egg
2½ cups Pillsbury's BEST® All Purpose or Unbleached Flour
½ teaspoon cream of tartar
½ teaspoon baking soda
¼ teaspoon salt
   Yellow decorator sugar

In large bowl, beat sugar, powdered sugar, butter and oil until light and fluffy. Add lemon peel, lemon juice and egg; blend well. Lightly spoon flour into measuring cup; level off. Stir in flour, cream of tartar, baking soda and salt; mix well. Cover with plastic wrap; refrigerate 1 hour for easier handling.

Heat oven to 350°F. Shape dough into 1-inch balls; roll in decorator sugar. Place 2 inches apart on ungreased cookie sheets. Bake at 350°F. for 7 to 12 minutes or until set. Immediately remove from cookie sheets. 3½ dozen cookies.

HIGH ALTITUDE – Above 3500 Feet: Decrease sugar to ⅓ cup. Increase flour to 2¾ cups. Bake as directed above.

NUTRITION INFORMATION

SERVING SIZE: 1 COOKIE		PERCENT U.S. RDA PER SERVING	
CALORIES	90	PROTEIN	*
PROTEIN	1 g	VITAMIN A	2%
CARBOHYDRATE	11 g	VITAMIN C	*
FAT	5 g	THIAMINE	4%
CHOLESTEROL	14 mg	RIBOFLAVIN	2%
SODIUM	60 mg	NIACIN	2%
POTASSIUM	10 mg	CALCIUM	*
		IRON	2%

* Contains less than 2% of the U.S. RDA of this nutrient.

Fully ripened bananas provide the best flavor for these cookies. You'll love the creamy, melt-in-your-mouth flavor combination.

⬥

CARAMEL FROSTED BANANA DROPS

COOKIES
1 cup firmly packed brown sugar
1 cup margarine or butter, softened
½ cup (1 large) mashed banana
2 teaspoons vanilla
2⅓ cups Pillsbury's BEST® All Purpose or Unbleached Flour
¼ teaspoon salt
¾ cup chopped walnuts or pecans

FROSTING
¾ cup firmly packed brown sugar
¼ cup margarine or butter, softened
1¼ cups powdered sugar
½ teaspoon vanilla
1 to 3 tablespoons milk

Heat oven to 350°F. In large bowl, beat 1 cup brown sugar and 1 cup margarine until light and fluffy. Add banana and 2 teaspoons vanilla; blend well. Lightly spoon flour into measuring cup; level off. Stir in flour and salt; mix well. Stir in walnuts. Drop dough by rounded teaspoonfuls 2 inches apart onto ungreased cookie sheets.

Bake at 350°F. for 9 to 14 minutes or until light golden brown. Immediately remove from cookie sheets. Cool completely.

In small saucepan, combine ¾ cup brown sugar and ¼ cup margarine. Cook over medium heat until sugar is dissolved, stirring constantly. Cool slightly. Stir in powdered sugar, ½ teaspoon vanilla and enough milk for desired spreading consistency.* Frost cooled cookies.
5 dozen cookies.

TIP:

* If frosting begins to thicken while using, stir in additional milk, one teaspoon at a time.

HIGH ALTITUDE – Above 3500 Feet: Decrease brown sugar in cookies to ¾ cup. Increase flour to 2⅔ cups. Bake as directed above.

NUTRITION INFORMATION

SERVING SIZE: 1 COOKIE		PERCENT U.S. RDA PER SERVING	
CALORIES	100	PROTEIN	*
PROTEIN	1 g	VITAMIN A	2%
CARBOHYDRATE	13 g	VITAMIN C	*
FAT	5 g	THIAMINE	2%
CHOLESTEROL	0 mg	RIBOFLAVIN	*
SODIUM	55 mg	NIACIN	*
POTASSIUM	45 mg	CALCIUM	*
		IRON	2%

* Contains less than 2% of the U.S. RDA of this nutrient.

You'll notice that these cookies have no sugar in the dough. The sweetness comes from dipping the cookies in sugar and from the mints baked in the center. They are delicious served with coffee or tea. Store the cookies tightly covered.

SANDWICHED MINT SURPRISES

2 cups Pillsbury's BEST® All
　　Purpose or Unbleached
　　Flour
1 cup margarine or butter,
　　softened
⅓ cup half-and-half
3 tablespoons unsweetened
　　cocoa
½ teaspoon vanilla
　　Sugar
36 thin pastel wafer mints

Heat oven to 375°F. Lightly grease cookie sheets. Lightly spoon flour into measuring cup; level off. In large bowl, combine flour, margarine, half-and-half, cocoa and vanilla. Beat at low speed until well mixed, scraping sides of bowl frequently. Cover with plastic wrap; refrigerate 30 minutes or until dough is firm enough to roll.

On lightly floured surface, roll half of dough to ⅛-inch thickness; refrigerate remaining dough. Cut with lightly floured 2-inch round cookie cutter. Dip 1 side of each dough round in sugar. Place half of dough rounds, sugared side down, on greased cookie sheets. Place mint wafer in center of each dough round. Top each with second dough round, sugared side up. Press fork firmly around edges of each to seal. Repeat with remaining dough, sugar and mints.

Bake at 375°F. for 8 to 10 minutes or until set. Cool 1 minute; remove from cookie sheets. Cool completely.
3 dozen cookies.

HIGH ALTITUDE – Above 3500 Feet: No change.

NUTRITION INFORMATION

SERVING SIZE: 1 COOKIE		PERCENT U.S. RDA PER SERVING	
CALORIES	100	PROTEIN	*
PROTEIN	1 g	VITAMIN A	4%
CARBOHYDRATE	11 g	VITAMIN C	*
FAT	6 g	THIAMINE	4%
CHOLESTEROL	1 mg	RIBOFLAVIN	2%
SODIUM	75 mg	NIACIN	2%
POTASSIUM	15 mg	CALCIUM	*
		IRON	2%

* Contains less than 2% of the U.S. RDA of this nutrient.

This refrigerator cookie dough stores well. Cookies can be baked up to several days after preparing and shaping the dough. For best results, use a sharp knife to slice the cookies.

CRANBERRY AND ORANGE PINWHEELS

(pictured on right)

FILLING
1 tablespoon cornstarch
¾ cup whole berry cranberry
   sauce
¼ cup orange marmalade

COOKIES
¾ cup firmly packed brown
   sugar
½ cup margarine or butter,
   softened
1 egg
1¾ cups Pillsbury's BEST® All
   Purpose or Unbleached
   Flour
1 teaspoon baking powder
1 teaspoon grated orange peel
¼ teaspoon salt
¼ teaspoon allspice

In small saucepan, combine all filling ingredients. Bring to a boil over medium heat, stirring constantly. Refrigerate until thoroughly chilled.

In large bowl, beat brown sugar, margarine and egg until light and fluffy. Lightly spoon flour into measuring cup; level off. Stir in flour, baking powder, orange peel, salt and allspice; mix well. Cover with plastic wrap; refrigerate 1 hour for easier handling.

On lightly floured surface, roll dough into 16x8-inch rectangle. Spoon and spread cooled filling evenly over dough to within ½ inch of edges. Starting with 16-inch side, roll up jelly-roll fashion; cut in half to form two 8-inch rolls. Wrap tightly in plastic wrap or waxed paper; freeze at least 2 hours.

Heat oven to 375°F. Generously grease cookie sheets. Using sharp knife, cut dough into ½-inch thick slices. Place 2 inches apart on greased cookie sheets. Bake at 375°F. for 9 to 13 minutes or until light golden brown. Immediately remove from cookie sheets. 3 dozen cookies.

HIGH ALTITUDE – Above 3500 Feet: Increase flour to 2 cups. Bake as directed above.

NUTRITION INFORMATION

SERVING SIZE: 1 COOKIE		PERCENT U.S. RDA PER SERVING	
CALORIES	80	PROTEIN	*
PROTEIN	1 g	VITAMIN A	2%
CARBOHYDRATE	13 g	VITAMIN C	*
FAT	3 g	THIAMINE	2%
CHOLESTEROL	6 mg	RIBOFLAVIN	2%
SODIUM	60 mg	NIACIN	*
POTASSIUM	30 mg	CALCIUM	*
		IRON	2%

* Contains less than 2% of the U.S. RDA of this nutrient.

Cranberry and Orange Pinwheels,
Granola Apple Cookies **p. 42**

These soft-textured cookies with lots of healthful ingredients are delicious glazed or unglazed. Store them between sheets of waxed paper in a tightly covered container.

GRANOLA APPLE COOKIES

(pictured on p. 41)

COOKIES
1½ cups firmly packed brown
    sugar
½ cup margarine or butter,
    softened
¼ cup milk
1 tablespoon lemon juice
1 teaspoon grated lemon peel
1 egg
1½ cups Pillsbury's BEST® All
    Purpose or Unbleached
    Flour
1 cup Pillsbury's BEST® Whole
    Wheat Flour
1 teaspoon baking soda
1 teaspoon cinnamon or
    nutmeg
¼ teaspoon salt
1½ cups finely chopped apples
1 cup granola
1 cup chopped walnuts or
    pecans

GLAZE
¾ cup powdered sugar
2 to 3 teaspoons lemon juice

Heat oven to 375°F. In large bowl, beat brown sugar and margarine until light and fluffy. Add milk, 1 tablespoon lemon juice, lemon peel and egg; blend well. Lightly spoon flour into measuring cup; level off. Stir in all purpose flour, whole wheat flour, baking soda, cinnamon and salt; mix well. Stir in apples, granola and walnuts. Drop dough by heaping teaspoonfuls 2 inches apart onto ungreased cookie sheets.

Bake at 375°F. for 9 to 13 minutes or until light golden brown. Immediately remove from cookie sheets. Cool completely.

In small bowl, combine glaze ingredients, adding enough lemon juice for desired drizzling consistency. Drizzle over cooled cookies. 3 dozen cookies.

HIGH ALTITUDE – Above 3500 Feet: Decrease brown sugar to 1 cup. Bake as directed above.

NUTRITION INFORMATION

SERVING SIZE: 1 COOKIE		PERCENT U.S. RDA PER SERVING	
CALORIES	140	PROTEIN	2%
PROTEIN	2 g	VITAMIN A	2%
CARBOHYDRATE	21 g	VITAMIN C	*
FAT	6 g	THIAMINE	6%
CHOLESTEROL	6 mg	RIBOFLAVIN	2%
SODIUM	80 mg	NIACIN	2%
POTASSIUM	95 mg	CALCIUM	*
		IRON	4%

* Contains less than 2% of the U.S. RDA of this nutrient.

Apples and raisins are teamed with nuts and whole wheat flour in this chewy, wholesome cookie.

CIDER NUT COOKIES

1 cup firmly packed brown sugar
½ cup margarine or butter, softened
¼ cup apple cider or apple juice
2 eggs
1½ cups Pillsbury's BEST® All Purpose or Unbleached Flour
½ cup Pillsbury's BEST® Whole Wheat Flour
1 teaspoon baking soda
¼ teaspoon salt
1 teaspoon cinnamon
½ teaspoon nutmeg
1 cup chopped nuts
1 cup diced peeled apple
½ cup raisins

Heat oven to 375°F. Grease cookie sheets. In large bowl, beat brown sugar and margarine until light and fluffy. Add apple cider and eggs; blend well. Lightly spoon flour into measuring cup; level off. Stir in all purpose flour, whole wheat flour, baking soda, salt, cinnamon and nutmeg; mix well. Stir in nuts, apple and raisins. Drop dough by teaspoonfuls 2 inches apart onto greased cookie sheets.

Bake at 375°F. for 8 to 12 minutes or until golden brown. Immediately remove from cookie sheets.
4 dozen cookies.

HIGH ALTITUDE - Above 3500 Feet: No change.

NUTRITION INFORMATION

SERVING SIZE: 1 COOKIE		PERCENT U.S. RDA PER SERVING	
CALORIES	80	PROTEIN	*
PROTEIN	1 g	VITAMIN A	*
CARBOHYDRATE	11 g	VITAMIN C	*
FAT	4 g	THIAMINE	2%
CHOLESTEROL	9 mg	RIBOFLAVIN	2%
SODIUM	60 mg	NIACIN	*
POTASSIUM	60 mg	CALCIUM	*
		IRON	2%

* Contains less than 2% of the U.S. RDA of this nutrient.

These easy-to-make chewy chocolate cookies are one of our most requested recipes. Once you taste them, you'll understand why! The recipe was developed for those of you requesting an easy cookie made from a cake mix. The cookies puff during baking and then settle when removed from the oven, forming a pretty crinkled top.

GERMAN CHOCOLATE CAKE MIX COOKIES

1 pkg. Pillsbury Plus® German Chocolate Cake Mix
1 (6-oz.) pkg. (1 cup) semi-sweet chocolate chips
½ cup rolled oats
½ cup raisins
½ cup oil
2 eggs, slightly beaten

Heat oven to 350°F. In large bowl, combine all ingredients; blend well. Drop dough by rounded teaspoonfuls 2 inches apart onto ungreased cookie sheets.

Bake at 350°F. for 8 to 10 minutes or until set. Cool 1 minute; remove from cookie sheets. 4½ dozen cookies.

HIGH ALTITUDE - Above 3500 Feet: Add ¼ cup flour to dry cake mix. Bake as directed above.

NUTRITION INFORMATION

SERVING SIZE: 1 COOKIE		PERCENT U.S. RDA PER SERVING	
CALORIES	80	PROTEIN	*
PROTEIN	1 g	VITAMIN A	*
CARBOHYDRATE	11 g	VITAMIN C	*
FAT	4 g	THIAMINE	2%
CHOLESTEROL	8 mg	RIBOFLAVIN	*
SODIUM	60 mg	NIACIN	*
POTASSIUM	35 mg	CALCIUM	*
		IRON	*

* Contains less than 2% of the U.S. RDA of this nutrient.

Children will delight in making a variety of faces on these frosted cookies.

———— ❁ ————

MOLASSES JACK-O-LANTERN COOKIES

(pictured on left)

COOKIES
1 cup sugar
½ cup margarine or butter, softened
⅓ cup molasses
1 egg
2 cups Pillsbury's BEST® All Purpose or Unbleached Flour
2 teaspoons grated orange peel
1½ teaspoons baking soda
1 teaspoon cinnamon
½ teaspoon ginger
¼ teaspoon salt
¼ teaspoon cloves

ICING
Buttery Decorator Icing (page 46)
3 drops red food color
6 drops yellow food color
4 drops green food color
Miniature chocolate chips
Candy corn
Gumdrops

In large bowl, beat sugar and margarine until light and fluffy. Add molasses and egg; blend well. Lightly spoon flour into measuring cup; level off. Stir in flour and remaining cookie ingredients; mix well. Cover with plastic wrap; refrigerate 1 to 3 hours for easier handling.

Heat oven to 350°F. On well-floured surface, roll half of dough to ⅛-inch thickness. Cut with floured 3-inch pumpkin-shaped or round cookie cutter. Place 1 inch apart on ungreased cookie sheets. Repeat with remaining half of dough.

Bake at 350°F. for 6 to 9 minutes or until set. Immediately remove from cookie sheets.

In small bowl, combine half of Buttery Decorator Icing, 3 drops red food color and 3 drops of the yellow food color; blend well to make orange icing. Divide remaining icing mixture in half; place in 2 small bowls. Add 4 drops green food color to 1 bowl and remaining 3 drops yellow food color to second bowl; blend each well. To decorate cookies, frost each cookie with orange-colored icing. Use green and yellow icings, chocolate chips, candy corn and gumdrops to make faces on frosted cookies. 24 cookies.

HIGH ALTITUDE – Above 3500 Feet: Decrease sugar to ⅔ cup. Increase flour to 2½ cups. Bake as directed above.

NUTRITION INFORMATION

SERVING SIZE: 1 COOKIE		PERCENT U.S. RDA PER SERVING	
CALORIES	220	PROTEIN	*
PROTEIN	1 g	VITAMIN A	4%
CARBOHYDRATE	35 g	VITAMIN C	*
FAT	9 g	THIAMINE	4%
CHOLESTEROL	16 mg	RIBOFLAVIN	2%
SODIUM	160 mg	NIACIN	2%
POTASSIUM	65 mg	CALCIUM	*
		IRON	4%

* Contains less than 2% of the U.S. RDA of this nutrient.

Molasses Jack-O-Lantern Cookies

This delicious, creamy icing is wonderful for frosting cookies, cakes or bars. We've used it to frost **Molasses Jack-O-Lantern Cookies** *(page 45) and we know that once you've tried it, you'll use it again and again.*

BUTTERY DECORATOR ICING

½ cup butter or margarine, softened
¼ cup shortening
1 teaspoon vanilla
⅛ teaspoon salt
4 cups powdered sugar
2 to 4 tablespoons milk

In large bowl, beat butter and shortening until light and fluffy. Add vanilla and salt. Beat in powdered sugar 1 cup at a time, scraping down sides of bowl. Add 2 tablespoons milk; beat at high speed until light and fluffy. Add enough additional milk for desired spreading consistency. 3 cups.

TIP:

This icing can be made up to 2 weeks in advance and stored in airtight container in refrigerator. Bring to room temperature and rewhip before using.

NUTRITION INFORMATION

SERVING SIZE: 1 TABLESPOON		PERCENT U.S. RDA PER SERVING	
CALORIES	70	PROTEIN	*
PROTEIN	0 g	VITAMIN A	*
CARBOHYDRATE	10 g	VITAMIN C	*
FAT	3 g	THIAMINE	*
CHOLESTEROL	5 mg	RIBOFLAVIN	*
SODIUM	25 mg	NIACIN	*
POTASSIUM	0 mg	CALCIUM	*
		IRON	*

* Contains less than 2% of the U.S. RDA of this nutrient.

Use your choice of candy coating or white baking bar to create these delectable candy-filled party cookies.

WHITE-CAPPED MOCHA COOKIES

COOKIES
½ cup firmly packed brown sugar
¼ cup sugar
½ cup margarine or butter, softened
1 (8-oz.) pkg. cream cheese, softened, reserving 2 oz. for frosting
2 teaspoons instant coffee granules or crystals
2 teaspoons hot water
1 egg
2 cups Pillsbury's BEST® All Purpose or Unbleached Flour
¼ cup unsweetened cocoa
1 teaspoon baking powder

FILLING
2 to 3 oz. vanilla-flavored candy coating or white baking bar, cut into small pieces (about ¼-inch cubes)

FROSTING
1 cup powdered sugar
Reserved 2 oz. cream cheese
2 to 3 teaspoons milk

Heat oven to 350°F. In large bowl, beat brown sugar, sugar, margarine and 6 oz. of the cream cheese until light and fluffy. In small bowl, dissolve instant coffee in hot water. Add dissolved coffee and egg; blend well. Lightly spoon flour into measuring cup; level off. Stir in flour, cocoa and baking powder; mix well. Shape level tablespoonful dough around small chunk of candy coating, covering completely. Place 2 inches apart on ungreased cookie sheets.

Bake at 350°F. for 8 to 11 minutes. Cool 1 minute; remove from cookie sheets. Cool completely.

In small bowl, combine all frosting ingredients, adding enough milk for desired spreading consistency. Frost cooled cookies. 4½ dozen cookies.

HIGH ALTITUDE – Above 3500 Feet: Decrease baking powder to ½ teaspoon. Bake as directed above.

NUTRITION INFORMATION

SERVING SIZE: 1 COOKIE		PERCENT U.S. RDA PER SERVING	
CALORIES	80	PROTEIN	*
PROTEIN	1 g	VITAMIN A	2%
CARBOHYDRATE	10 g	VITAMIN C	*
FAT	4 g	THIAMINE	2%
CHOLESTEROL	9 mg	RIBOFLAVIN	2%
SODIUM	45 mg	NIACIN	*
POTASSIUM	30 mg	CALCIUM	*
		IRON	2%

* Contains less than 2% of the U.S. RDA of this nutrient.

These drop cookies transform into lovely lacy rounds during baking. Topped with a chocolate drizzle, they are a special occasion cookie indeed.

LACY OATMEAL FLORENTINES

COOKIES

½ **cup sugar**
   Dash salt
½ **cup butter or margarine,**
   softened
½ **teaspoon vanilla**
1½ **cups quick-cooking rolled**
   oats

GLAZE

¼ **cup semi-sweet chocolate**
   chips
2 **tablespoons butter or**
   margarine

Heat oven to 375°F. Grease cookie sheets. In small bowl, beat sugar, salt, ½ cup butter and vanilla until light and fluffy. Stir in oats; mix well. (Dough will be crumbly.) Drop dough by teaspoonfuls 2 inches apart onto greased cookie sheets; flatten slightly.

Bake at 375°F. for 4 to 6 minutes or until edges are golden brown. Cool 2 minutes; remove from cookie sheets. Cool completely.

In small saucepan, melt glaze ingredients over low heat, stirring constantly. Drizzle over cooled cookies. 3 dozen cookies.

HIGH ALTITUDE – Above 3500 Feet: Add 1 tablespoon flour with rolled oats. Bake as directed above.

NUTRITION INFORMATION

SERVING SIZE: 1 COOKIE		PERCENT U.S. RDA PER SERVING	
CALORIES	60	PROTEIN	*
PROTEIN	1 g	VITAMIN A	2%
CARBOHYDRATE	6 g	VITAMIN C	*
FAT	4 g	THIAMINE	*
CHOLESTEROL	9 mg	RIBOFLAVIN	*
SODIUM	35 mg	NIACIN	*
POTASSIUM	15 mg	CALCIUM	*
		IRON	*

* Contains less than 2% of the U.S. RDA of this nutrient.

BROWNIES

Tantalize with these irresistible creations!

An American invention and tradition, brownies can be as varied as the people who eat and enjoy them. If you like your brownies cake-like and mildly chocolaty, try **German Chocolate Saucepan Brownies**, complete with a chewy broiled topping. For those of you desiring a dense, rich variety, we recommend **Brazil Nut Brownies**. Frosted with creamy white chocolate, they will satisfy any chocolate craving. Blond brownies are special without chocolate. One of our favorites, **Date Pecan Blondies**, is a melt-in-your-mouth treat flavored with dates, brown sugar and nutmeg.

Pictured:
PUMPKIN PATCH BROWNIES, page 50
CHOCOLATE COOKIE MICE, page 26

This whimsical special-occasion treat is especially easy to make with Pillsbury Fudge Brownie Mix and ready to spread frosting.

PUMPKIN PATCH BROWNIES

BROWNIES
- 1 (21½-oz.) pkg. **Pillsbury Fudge Brownie Mix**
- 1 teaspoon cinnamon
- ½ cup water
- ½ cup oil
- 1 egg

FROSTING
- 1 can **Pillsbury Chocolate Fudge Frosting Supreme**™
- 1 cup **Pillsbury Vanilla Frosting Supreme**®
- 3 to 4 drops green food coloring
- 24 candy pumpkins

Heat oven to 350°F. Line 13x9-inch pan with foil, leaving enough foil on sides to lift brownies out of pan. Grease foil. In large bowl, combine all brownie ingredients; beat 50 strokes by hand. Spread in foil-lined pan.

Bake at 350°F. for 28 to 35 minutes. DO NOT OVERBAKE. Cool completely. Remove brownies from pan by lifting foil edges. Invert onto serving plate, tray or heavy cardboard covered with foil. Remove foil from brownies. Frost sides and top with chocolate fudge frosting. With knife, score frosting into 24 bars.

In small bowl, combine vanilla frosting and green food color; blend well. Using decorator bag, decorating bottle, or resealable plastic bag with a small cut in one corner, pipe green frosting to make vine and leaf design on each bar. Place candy pumpkin on each bar. Refrigerate 1 to 2 hours or until frosting is firm; cut into bars. 24 bars.

VARIATION:
PUMPKIN FIELD BROWNIES: Prepare brownies and frost with chocolate fudge frosting as directed above. Do not score. Prepare green frosting as directed above. Pipe vines and leaves randomly over chocolate fudge frosting. Place desired number of candy pumpkins randomly among leaves and vines.

HIGH ALTITUDE – Above 3500 Feet: Add ¼ cup flour to dry brownie mix. Bake as directed above.

NUTRITION INFORMATION

SERVING SIZE: 1 BAR		PERCENT U.S. RDA PER SERVING	
CALORIES	340	PROTEIN	2%
PROTEIN	2 g	VITAMIN A	*
CARBOHYDRATE	54 g	VITAMIN C	*
FAT	13 g	THIAMINE	2%
CHOLESTEROL	9 mg	RIBOFLAVIN	2%
SODIUM	190 mg	NIACIN	2%
POTASSIUM	125 mg	CALCIUM	*
		IRON	4%

* Contains less than 2% of the U.S. RDA of this nutrient.

Cook's Note

DETERMINING BROWNIE DONENESS

Brownies should not be overbaked but it is not always easy to tell when they're done. Each recipe provides a baking time range and with the following tips you will be able to more easily determine brownie doneness:

- Brownies will just begin to pull away from the sides of the pan.

- The top of the brownies will appear dry but shiny.

- The top of the brownies will be slightly cracked.

- Brownies will be firm to the touch in the center.

- A toothpick inserted in the center will come out with a moist crumb on it.

Children will love seeing their favorite turtle cartoon characters atop these chewy brownies.

COOKIE-TOPPED MICROWAVE BROWNIES

BROWNIES
1 (10.65-oz.) pkg. Pillsbury
    Microwave Fudge Brownie
    Mix
⅓ cup hot water
¼ cup oil

TOPPING
⅓ cup butterscotch or peanut
    butter-flavored chips
1 teaspoon oil
18 miniature turtle-shaped
    cookies

MICROWAVE DIRECTIONS:
In medium bowl, combine all brownie ingredients. Stir 50 strokes by hand or until well blended. Spread batter evenly in ungreased Pillsbury 7-inch square microwave pan.

Microwave on HIGH for 2 minutes. Rotate one-half turn (including ovens with turntables). Microwave an additional 2 minutes (or 3 minutes in compact ovens under 600 watts). Brownies are done when top surface loses almost all of wet appearance in center. If brownies are not done, continue microwaving in 30-second intervals. Place on heat-proof counter.

In small microwave-safe bowl, combine butterscotch chips and 1 teaspoon oil. Microwave on MEDIUM for 2 to 3 minutes or until melted, stirring once halfway through cooking. Spread over warm brownies; score into 9 bars. Top each bar with two turtle cookies. Cool 15 minutes. Cut through scored lines into bars. 9 bars.

HIGH ALTITUDE – Above 3500 Feet: Add 1 tablespoon flour to dry mix and reduce oil in brownies to 2 tablespoons. Microwave as directed above.

Mint candies are used to create an easy swirled frosting on these delicately flavored brownies.

CANDY MINT-TOPPED BROWNIES

1 (21½-oz.) pkg. Pillsbury Fudge
    Brownie Mix
½ cup water
½ cup oil
1 teaspoon mint extract
1 egg
1 (6-oz.) pkg. foil-wrapped
    rectangular chocolate mints,
    unwrapped

Heat oven to 350°F. Grease 13x9-inch pan. In large bowl, combine brownie mix, water, oil, mint extract and egg; beat 50 strokes by hand. Spread in greased pan.

Bake at 350°F. for 28 to 35 minutes. DO NOT OVERBAKE. Immediately arrange chocolate mints evenly over brownies. Let stand 5 minutes or until mints are softened. Using knife or spatula, spread gently, swirling chocolate mints slightly. Cool completely; cut into bars. 36 bars.

HIGH ALTITUDE – Above 3500 Feet: Add ¼ cup flour to dry brownie mix. Bake as directed above.

What could be more delicious than white chocolate frosting atop fudgy brownies? When melting the white baking bar, use a clean, dry saucepan. Even the smallest amount of moisture can cause the chocolate to become thick, lumpy and grainy during melting. We've added a small amount of oil to ensure smooth melting. Be sure to stir constantly while the bar is melting.

BRAZIL NUT BROWNIES

(pictured on right)

BROWNIES
- 1 (21½-oz.) pkg. Pillsbury Fudge Brownie Mix
- ½ cup oil
- ¼ cup water
- ¼ cup coffee-flavored liqueur or strong coffee
- 1 egg
- 1 cup coarsely chopped brazil nuts

FROSTING
- 2 tablespoons margarine or butter, melted
- 1 cup powdered sugar
- 2 tablespoons coffee-flavored liqueur or strong coffee
- 1 tablespoon water
- 3 oz. white baking bar or ½ cup vanilla milk chips
- 1 tablespoon oil

Heat oven to 350°F. Grease 13x9-inch pan. In large bowl, combine all brownie ingredients except nuts; beat 50 strokes by hand. Stir in brazil nuts. Spread in greased pan. Bake at 350°F. for 28 to 35 minutes. DO NOT OVERBAKE. Cool completely.

In medium bowl, combine margarine, powdered sugar, 2 tablespoons liqueur and 1 tablespoon water; blend well. In small saucepan over low heat, melt white baking bar and oil, stirring constantly. Add to powdered sugar mixture; beat until smooth. Spread over cooled

brownies. Let stand until set. Cut into bars. 36 bars.

HIGH ALTITUDE – Above 3500 Feet: Add ¼ cup flour to dry brownie mix. Bake as directed above.

NUTRITION INFORMATION

SERVING SIZE: 1 BAR		PERCENT U.S. RDA PER SERVING	
CALORIES	170	PROTEIN	2%
PROTEIN	2 g	VITAMIN A	*
CARBOHYDRATE	20 g	VITAMIN C	*
FAT	9 g	THIAMINE	4%
CHOLESTEROL	6 mg	RIBOFLAVIN	2%
SODIUM	70 mg	NIACIN	*
POTASSIUM	70 mg	CALCIUM	*
		IRON	2%

* Contains less than 2% of the U.S. RDA of this nutrient.

No need to frost these wonderful fruit-filled brownies—they are temptingly delicious just as they are. Because the brownies have a lower fat and calorie count, everyone will be able to enjoy at least one!

TANGY ORANGE AND FRUIT BROWNIES

- 1 (19.85-oz.) pkg. Pillsbury Lovin' Lites™ Fudge Brownie Mix
- 1 tablespoon grated orange peel
- ⅓ cup orange juice
- 2 egg whites
- 1 (6-oz.) pkg. dried fruit bits

Heat oven to 350°F. Grease 13x9-inch pan with no-stick cooking spray or solid shortening. In large bowl, combine brownie mix, orange peel, orange juice and egg whites; stir 75 strokes by hand. Stir in fruit bits. Spread in greased pan.

Bake at 350°F. for 28 to 30 minutes. DO NOT OVERBAKE. Cool completely; cut into bars. 24 bars.

HIGH ALTITUDE – Above 3500 Feet: Add ¼ cup flour to dry brownie mix. Bake as directed above.

NUTRITION INFORMATION

SERVING SIZE: 1 BAR		PERCENT U.S. RDA PER SERVING	
CALORIES	120	PROTEIN	2%
PROTEIN	1 g	VITAMIN A	*
CARBOHYDRATE	23 g	VITAMIN C	2%
FAT	2 g	THIAMINE	2%
CHOLESTEROL	0 mg	RIBOFLAVIN	2%
SODIUM	85 mg	NIACIN	2%
POTASSIUM	115 mg	CALCIUM	*
		IRON	2%

* Contains less than 2% of the U.S. RDA of this nutrient.

Serve these brownies for a special adult occasion! Bourbon is drizzled over the brownies while they're warm, adding a distinctive flavor.

BEST EVER BOURBON BROWNIES

BROWNIES
½ **cup sugar**
⅓ **cup margarine or butter**
2 **tablespoons water**
1 **(6-oz.) pkg. (1 cup) semi-sweet chocolate chips**
1 **teaspoon vanilla**
2 **eggs**
¾ **cup Pillsbury's BEST® All Purpose or Unbleached Flour**
¼ **teaspoon baking powder**
¼ **teaspoon salt**
½ **cup chopped walnuts or pecans**
3 **to 4 tablespoons bourbon**

FROSTING
1½ **cups powdered sugar**
3 **tablespoons margarine or butter, softened**
¼ **teaspoon vanilla**
2 **to 3 teaspoons milk**
1 **oz. (1 square) semi-sweet chocolate, melted, cooled**

Heat oven to 350°F. Grease 8 or 9-inch square pan. In medium saucepan, combine sugar, ⅓ cup margarine and water. Cook over medium heat until mixture comes to a boil, stirring constantly. Remove from heat; stir in chocolate chips and 1 teaspoon vanilla. Add eggs; beat well. Lightly spoon flour into measuring cup; level off. Add flour, baking powder and salt; mix well. Stir in walnuts. Spread evenly in greased pan.

Bake at 350°F. for 20 to 30 minutes or until toothpick inserted in center comes out clean. DO NOT OVERBAKE. Drizzle bourbon evenly over top. Cool completely.

In small bowl, combine powdered sugar, 3 tablespoons margarine, ¼ teaspoon vanilla and enough milk for desired frosting consistency; beat until smooth. Frost cooled brownies; drizzle melted chocolate over frosting. Let stand until set; cut into bars. 24 bars.

HIGH ALTITUDE – Above 3500 Feet: Increase flour to ¾ cup plus 2 tablespoons. Bake as directed above.

NUTRITION INFORMATION

SERVING SIZE: 1 BAR		PERCENT U.S. RDA PER SERVING	
CALORIES	160	PROTEIN	2%
PROTEIN	2 g	VITAMIN A	4%
CARBOHYDRATE	20 g	VITAMIN C	*
FAT	9 g	THIAMINE	2%
CHOLESTEROL	18 mg	RIBOFLAVIN	2%
SODIUM	75 mg	NIACIN	*
POTASSIUM	50 mg	CALCIUM	*
		IRON	2%

* Contains less than 2% of the U.S. RDA of this nutrient.

These delicious cake-like brownies are a breeze to make. Ingredients are mixed together quickly in one bowl. A delectable cocoa frosting completes them.

CHOCOLATE SYRUP PECAN BROWNIES

BROWNIES
1 cup sugar
½ cup margarine or butter, softened
1 tablespoon vanilla
3 eggs
1 (16-oz.) can chocolate-flavored syrup
1¼ cups Pillsbury's BEST® All Purpose or Unbleached Flour
½ cup finely chopped pecans

FROSTING
¼ cup margarine or butter
¼ cup unsweetened cocoa
1½ cups powdered sugar
½ teaspoon vanilla
2 to 3 tablespoons milk
½ cup finely chopped pecans

Heat oven to 350°F. Grease 13x9-inch pan. In large bowl, beat sugar and ½ cup margarine until light and fluffy. Add 1 tablespoon vanilla, eggs and chocolate syrup; blend well. Lightly spoon flour into measuring cup; level off. Add flour; mix well. Stir in ½ cup chopped pecans. Spread in greased pan.

Bake at 350°F. for 30 to 35 minutes or until toothpick inserted in center comes out clean. Cool completely.

Melt ¼ cup margarine in medium saucepan over medium heat. Blend in cocoa; heat until mixture just comes to a boil, stirring constantly. Cool slightly. Stir in powdered sugar, ½ teaspoon vanilla and enough milk for desired spreading consistency; blend until smooth. Stir in ½ cup chopped pecans. Spread carefully over cooled brownies. Cool completely; cut into bars. 36 bars.

HIGH ALTITUDE – Above 3500 Feet: No change.

NUTRITION INFORMATION

SERVING SIZE: 1 BAR		PERCENT U.S. RDA PER SERVING	
CALORIES	140	PROTEIN	2%
PROTEIN	2 g	VITAMIN A	4%
CARBOHYDRATE	22 g	VITAMIN C	*
FAT	6 g	THIAMINE	2%
CHOLESTEROL	18 mg	RIBOFLAVIN	2%
SODIUM	65 mg	NIACIN	*
POTASSIUM	55 mg	CALCIUM	*
		IRON	2%

* Contains less than 2% of the U.S. RDA of this nutrient.

Cook's Note

STORING COOKIES, BROWNIES AND BARS

For best results:

■ Store each kind of cookie in a separate container to prevent flavors from mixing.

■ To keep soft cookies soft, store them in a container with a tight-fitting cover. Place sheets of waxed paper between layers so the cookies will not stick together.

■ To keep crisp cookies crisp, store them in a container with a loose-fitting cover. However, if the weather is humid, use a tight-fitting cover.

■ To store brownies and bars, place them in a tightly covered container, or leave them right in the baking pan and cover it with a tight-fitting cover or foil.

We've kept the flavor but reduced the fat and sugar in this moist, chocolaty brownie.

CHOCO-LITE BROWNIES

⅔ cup Pillsbury's BEST® All
  Purpose or Unbleached
  Flour
¾ cup sugar
⅓ cup unsweetened cocoa
¼ teaspoon baking powder
¼ teaspoon salt
⅓ cup margarine, melted
2 teaspoons vanilla
2 eggs, slightly beaten
  Powdered sugar

Heat oven to 350°F. Grease and flour bottom only of 8-inch square pan. Lightly spoon flour into measuring cup; level off. In large bowl, combine flour, sugar, cocoa, baking powder and salt; blend well. Add margarine, vanilla and eggs; stir just to combine. Pour into greased and floured pan.

Bake at 350°F. for 18 to 23 minutes or until set. DO NOT OVERBAKE. Sprinkle with powdered sugar. Cool completely; cut into bars. 24 bars.

HIGH ALTITUDE – Above 3500 Feet: Increase flour to ¾ cup. Bake as directed above.

NUTRITION INFORMATION

SERVING SIZE: 1 BAR		PERCENT U.S. RDA PER SERVING	
CALORIES	70	PROTEIN	*
PROTEIN	1 g	VITAMIN A	2%
CARBOHYDRATE	10 g	VITAMIN C	*
FAT	3 g	THIAMINE	2%
CHOLESTEROL	18 mg	RIBOFLAVIN	2%
SODIUM	70 mg	NIACIN	*
POTASSIUM	20 mg	CALCIUM	*
		IRON	*

* Contains less than 2% of the U.S. RDA of this nutrient.

CHOCOLATE CHERRY MICROWAVE BROWNIES

(pictured on right)

1 (10.65-oz.) pkg. Pillsbury
  Microwave Fudge Brownie
  Mix
⅓ cup hot water
¼ cup oil
½ cup vanilla milk chips
¼ cup maraschino cherries, well
  drained, chopped

▥ MICROWAVE DIRECTIONS:
In medium bowl, combine brownie mix, water and oil. Stir 50 strokes by hand or until well blended. Spread batter evenly in ungreased Pillsbury 7-inch square microwave pan.

Microwave on HIGH for 2 minutes. Rotate one-half turn (including ovens with turntables). Microwave an additional 2 minutes (or 3 minutes in compact ovens under 600 watts). Brownies are done when top surface loses almost all of wet appearance in center. If brownies are not done, continue microwaving in 30-second intervals. Place on heat-proof counter. Immediately sprinkle with vanilla milk chips; let stand 5 minutes or until chips are softened. If necessary, microwave brownies and chips on HIGH an additional 10 seconds to soften chips. Gently spread softened chips over brownies; sprinkle with cherries. Cool 15 minutes; cut into bars. 9 bars.

HIGH ALTITUDE – Above 3500 Feet: Add 1 tablespoon flour to dry mix and reduce oil to 2 tablespoons. Microwave as directed above.

NUTRITION INFORMATION

SERVING SIZE: 1 BAR		PERCENT U.S. RDA PER SERVING	
CALORIES	250	PROTEIN	4%
PROTEIN	3 g	VITAMIN A	*
CARBOHYDRATE	34 g	VITAMIN C	*
FAT	12 g	THIAMINE	4%
CHOLESTEROL	2 mg	RIBOFLAVIN	4%
SODIUM	120 mg	NIACIN	2%
POTASSIUM	160 mg	CALCIUM	2%
		IRON	6%

* Contains less than 2% of the U.S. RDA of this nutrient.

Almond paste is made from blanched ground almonds, sugar, liquid and sometimes almond extract. It contributes to the velvety texture of these elegant brownies.

ALMOND FUDGE BROWNIES

BROWNIES

1 teaspoon instant coffee
   granules or crystals
2 tablespoons hot water
4 eggs, separated
1 cup sugar
½ cup margarine or butter,
   softened
1 (3½-oz.) pkg. almond paste,
   crumbled into small pieces
1 cup Pillsbury's BEST® All
   Purpose or Unbleached
   Flour
1 (6-oz.) pkg. (1 cup) semi-
   sweet chocolate chips,
   melted
1 teaspoon vanilla
½ cup semi-sweet chocolate
   chips

FROSTING

¼ cup sugar
¼ cup firmly packed brown
   sugar
⅛ teaspoon salt
¼ cup milk
2 tablespoons margarine or
   butter
½ cup semi-sweet chocolate
   chips
1 cup powdered sugar
½ teaspoon vanilla

Heat oven to 350°F. Grease and flour bottom only of 13x9-inch pan. In small bowl, dissolve instant coffee in hot water. In another small bowl, beat egg whites until stiff peaks form.

In large bowl, beat 1 cup sugar and ½ cup margarine until light and fluffy. Stir in almond paste; blend well. Lightly spoon flour into measuring cup; level off. Add flour, dissolved coffee, egg yolks, melted chocolate chips and 1 teaspoon vanilla; mix well. Fold in beaten egg whites. Gently fold in ½ cup chocolate chips. Spread in greased and floured pan.

Bake at 350°F. for 25 to 35 minutes or until set. DO NOT OVERBAKE. Cool completely.

In small saucepan, combine ¼ cup sugar, brown sugar, salt, milk, 2 tablespoons margarine and ½ cup chocolate chips. Bring to a boil over medium heat, stirring constantly. Reduce heat; simmer 3 minutes. Remove from heat. Stir in powdered sugar and ½ teaspoon vanilla; beat until smooth. Frost cooled brownies; cut into bars. Store in refrigerator. 36 bars.

HIGH ALTITUDE – Above 3500 Feet: No change.

NUTRITION INFORMATION

SERVING SIZE: 1 BAR		PERCENT U.S. RDA PER SERVING	
CALORIES	160	PROTEIN	2%
PROTEIN	2 g	VITAMIN A	2%
CARBOHYDRATE	21 g	VITAMIN C	*
FAT	8 g	THIAMINE	2%
CHOLESTEROL	24 mg	RIBOFLAVIN	4%
SODIUM	55 mg	NIACIN	*
POTASSIUM	70 mg	CALCIUM	*
		IRON	2%

* Contains less than 2% of the U.S. RDA of this nutrient.

These brownies are dotted with crunchy cashews and then topped with a smooth, creamy frosting and more cashews. They're indescribably delicious!

FROSTED CASHEW BROWNIES

BROWNIES
1 (21½-oz.) pkg. Pillsbury Fudge
   Brownie Mix
½ cup water
½ cup oil
1 egg
½ cup coarsely chopped
   cashews

FROSTING
¼ cup margarine or butter
¼ cup unsweetened cocoa
1½ cups powdered sugar
1 teaspoon vanilla
2 to 3 tablespoons milk
½ cup cashew halves

Heat oven to 350°F. Grease 13x9-inch pan. In large bowl, combine brownie mix, water, oil and egg; beat 50 strokes by hand. Stir in chopped cashews. Spread in greased pan. Bake at 350°F. for 28 to 35 minutes. DO NOT OVERBAKE. Cool completely.

Melt margarine in medium saucepan over medium heat. Blend in cocoa; heat until mixture just comes to a boil, stirring constantly. Cool slightly. Stir in powdered sugar, vanilla and enough milk for desired spreading consistency; blend until smooth. Spread over cooled brownies; sprinkle with cashew halves. Cool completely; cut into bars. 36 bars.

HIGH ALTITUDE – Above 3500 Feet: Add ¼ cup flour to dry brownie mix. Bake as directed above.

NUTRITION INFORMATION

SERVING SIZE: 1 BAR		PERCENT U.S. RDA PER SERVING	
CALORIES	150	PROTEIN	2%
PROTEIN	2 g	VITAMIN A	*
CARBOHYDRATE	21 g	VITAMIN C	*
FAT	8 g	THIAMINE	2%
CHOLESTEROL	6 mg	RIBOFLAVIN	2%
SODIUM	105 mg	NIACIN	*
POTASSIUM	65 mg	CALCIUM	*
		IRON	4%

* Contains less than 2% of the U.S. RDA of this nutrient.

Absolutely delicious!

FRUITCAKE FANTASY BROWNIES

(pictured on right)

½ cup margarine or butter
4 oz. (4 squares) semi-sweet
    chocolate
1 (14-oz.) can sweetened
    condensed milk (not
    evaporated)
½ teaspoon rum extract
2 eggs
1¼ cups Pillsbury's BEST® All
    Purpose or Unbleached
    Flour
¾ teaspoon baking powder
¼ teaspoon salt
2 cups candied fruitcake
    mixture
1 cup chopped pecans or
    walnuts

Heat oven to 350°F. Grease 13x9-inch pan. In large saucepan, melt margarine and chocolate over low heat, stirring constantly. Remove from heat. Add sweetened condensed milk and rum extract; blend well. Add eggs 1 at a time, beating well after each addition. Lightly spoon flour into measuring cup; level off. Add flour, baking powder and salt; mix well. Stir in candied fruit and pecans. Spread in greased pan.

Bake at 350°F. for 28 to 36 minutes or until toothpick inserted in center comes out clean. Cool completely; cut into bars. 36 bars.

HIGH ALTITUDE – Above 3500 Feet: Increase flour to 1½ cups. Bake as directed above.

NUTRITION INFORMATION

SERVING SIZE: 1 BAR		PERCENT U.S. RDA PER SERVING	
CALORIES	160	PROTEIN	4%
PROTEIN	2 g	VITAMIN A	2%
CARBOHYDRATE	21 g	VITAMIN C	4%
FAT	7 g	THIAMINE	4%
CHOLESTEROL	17 mg	RIBOFLAVIN	6%
SODIUM	85 mg	NIACIN	*
POTASSIUM	115 mg	CALCIUM	6%
		IRON	2%

* Contains less than 2% of the U.S. RDA of this nutrient.

Date Pecan Blondies p. 62,
Fruitcake Fantasy Brownies

The term "blondie" refers to a brownie containing no chocolate. Our version of blond brownies is moist and chewy, with a rich melt-in-your-mouth flavor.

DATE PECAN BLONDIES

(pictured on p. 61)

1½ cups firmly packed brown
 sugar
½ cup margarine or butter,
 softened
2 teaspoons vanilla
2 eggs
1½ cups Pillsbury's BEST® All
 Purpose or Unbleached
 Flour
1 teaspoon baking powder
½ teaspoon nutmeg
¼ teaspoon salt
1 cup chopped dates
½ cup chopped pecans
1 tablespoon powdered sugar

Heat oven to 350°F. Grease 13x9-inch pan. In large bowl, beat brown sugar and margarine until light and fluffy. Add vanilla and eggs; blend well. Lightly spoon flour into measuring cup; level off. Add flour, baking powder, nutmeg and salt; mix well. Stir in dates. Spread in greased pan. Sprinkle with pecans.

Bake at 350°F. for 18 to 28 minutes or until set and golden brown. Cool completely. Sprinkle with powdered sugar; cut into bars. 36 bars.

HIGH ALTITUDE – Above 3500 Feet: Increase flour to 1¾ cups. Bake as directed above.

NUTRITION INFORMATION

SERVING SIZE: 1 BAR		PERCENT U.S. RDA PER SERVING	
CALORIES	110	PROTEIN	*
PROTEIN	1 g	VITAMIN A	2%
CARBOHYDRATE	17 g	VITAMIN C	*
FAT	4 g	THIAMINE	2%
CHOLESTEROL	12 mg	RIBOFLAVIN	2%
SODIUM	60 mg	NIACIN	2%
POTASSIUM	80 mg	CALCIUM	*
		IRON	4%

* Contains less than 2% of the U.S. RDA of this nutrient.

Fudgy brownies are enhanced with bananas and chocolate chips, and then topped with a wonderfully creamy pudding.

BANANA BROWNIES

BROWNIES

1 (21½-oz.) pkg. Pillsbury Fudge
 Brownie Mix
½ cup water
½ cup oil
1 egg
½ cup (1 medium) mashed
 banana
½ cup semi-sweet chocolate
 chips

TOPPING

1 (4-oz.) pkg. instant chocolate
 pudding and pie filling mix
1 cup dairy sour cream
¾ cup milk

Heat oven to 350°F. Grease 13x9-inch pan. In large bowl, combine brownie mix, water, oil and egg; beat 50 strokes by hand. Stir in mashed banana and chocolate chips. Spread in greased pan. Bake at 350°F. for 28 to 35 minutes. DO NOT OVERBAKE. Cool completely.

In medium bowl, combine topping ingredients; beat 1 minute or until thickened. Spread over cooled brownies. Garnish with banana slices dipped in lemon juice, if desired. Cut into bars. Store in refrigerator. 36 bars.

HIGH ALTITUDE – Above 3500 Feet: Add ¼ cup flour to dry brownie mix. Bake as directed above.

NUTRITION INFORMATION

SERVING SIZE: 1 BAR		PERCENT U.S. RDA PER SERVING	
CALORIES	140	PROTEIN	2%
PROTEIN	2 g	VITAMIN A	*
CARBOHYDRATE	19 g	VITAMIN C	*
FAT	7 g	THIAMINE	2%
CHOLESTEROL	9 mg	RIBOFLAVIN	2%
SODIUM	80 mg	NIACIN	*
POTASSIUM	75 mg	CALCIUM	2%
		IRON	2%

* Contains less than 2% of the U.S. RDA of this nutrient.

Delicate orange frosting complements these dense brownies. Hazelnuts, or filberts, add a distinctive flavor.

FUDGY ORANGE HAZELNUT BROWNIES

BROWNIES
1 cup sugar
½ cup margarine or butter, softened
⅓ cup unsweetened cocoa
1 tablespoon grated orange peel
2 eggs
1 cup Pillsbury's BEST® All Purpose or Unbleached Flour
½ teaspoon baking soda
¼ teaspoon salt
1 cup coarsely chopped hazelnuts

FROSTING
1 cup powdered sugar
1 teaspoon grated orange peel
1 to 2 tablespoons milk

Heat oven to 350°F. Grease 9-inch square pan. In large bowl, beat sugar and margarine until light and fluffy. Add cocoa, 1 tablespoon orange peel and eggs; blend well. Lightly spoon flour into measuring cup; level off. Add flour, baking soda and salt; mix well. Stir in hazelnuts. Spread in greased pan. Bake at 350°F. for 23 to 33 minutes or until firm to touch. DO NOT OVERBAKE. Cool completely.

In small bowl, combine powdered sugar, 1 teaspoon orange peel and enough milk for desired spreading consistency; blend until smooth. Spread over cooled brownies. Let stand until set; cut into bars. 24 bars.

HIGH ALTITUDE – Above 3500 Feet: Increase flour to 1¼ cups. Bake as directed above.

NUTRITION INFORMATION

SERVING SIZE: 1 BAR		PERCENT U.S. RDA PER SERVING	
CALORIES	140	PROTEIN	2%
PROTEIN	2 g	VITAMIN A	4%
CARBOHYDRATE	19 g	VITAMIN C	*
FAT	8 g	THIAMINE	4%
CHOLESTEROL	18 mg	RIBOFLAVIN	2%
SODIUM	105 mg	NIACIN	*
POTASSIUM	45 mg	CALCIUM	*
		IRON	2%

* Contains less than 2% of the U.S. RDA of this nutrient.

We all know s'mores are a warm, delicious combination of graham crackers, marshmallows and chocolate. This yummy recipe combines all these flavors in a crowd-sized pan of bars.

S'MORE BARS

BASE
1 (21½-oz.) pkg. Pillsbury Fudge Brownie Mix
¼ cup graham cracker crumbs
½ cup water
½ cup oil
1 egg

TOPPING
1 (6-oz.) pkg. (1 cup) semi-sweet chocolate chips
2 cups miniature marshmallows

Heat oven to 350°F. In large bowl, combine all base ingredients until moistened; beat 50 strokes by hand. Spread batter in ungreased 13x9-inch pan.

Bake at 350°F. for 30 to 35 minutes. DO NOT OVERBAKE. Remove from oven; set oven to broil. Immediately sprinkle bars with chocolate chips and marshmallows. Broil 4 to 6 inches from heat 1 minute or until marshmallows are puffy and slightly browned. Let stand until set. Cut into bars. 36 bars.

HIGH ALTITUDE – Above 3500 Feet: Add ¼ cup flour to dry brownie mix. Bake as directed above.

NUTRITION INFORMATION

SERVING SIZE: 1 BAR		PERCENT U.S. RDA PER SERVING	
CALORIES	130	PROTEIN	*
PROTEIN	1 g	VITAMIN A	*
CARBOHYDRATE	19 g	VITAMIN C	*
FAT	6 g	THIAMINE	2%
CHOLESTEROL	6 mg	RIBOFLAVIN	2%
SODIUM	65 mg	NIACIN	*
POTASSIUM	55 mg	CALCIUM	*
		IRON	2%

* Contains less than 2% of the U.S. RDA of this nutrient.

Sweet cooking chocolate is sometimes called German sweet chocolate. It is similar to semi-sweet chocolate but has a higher proportion of sugar. You'll find it packaged in 4-ounce bars.

GERMAN CHOCOLATE SAUCEPAN BROWNIES

(pictured on right)

BROWNIES
- ½ **cup margarine or butter**
- 1 **(4-oz.) bar sweet cooking chocolate, chopped**
- ½ **cup sugar**
- 1 **teaspoon vanilla**
- 2 **eggs**
- 1 **cup Pillsbury's BEST® All Purpose or Unbleached Flour**
- ½ **teaspoon baking powder**
- ¼ **teaspoon salt**

TOPPING
- 2 **tablespoons margarine or butter, melted**
- ½ **cup firmly packed brown sugar**
- 2 **tablespoons corn syrup**
- 2 **tablespoons milk**
- 1 **cup coconut**
- ½ **cup finely chopped pecans or walnuts**

Heat oven to 350°F. Grease 8- or 9-inch square pan. In medium saucepan, melt ½ cup margarine and chocolate over low heat, stirring constantly. Cool slightly. Add sugar and vanilla; blend well. Add eggs; beat well. Lightly spoon flour into measuring cup; level off. Add flour, baking powder and salt; mix well. Spread in greased pan.

Bake at 350°F. for 18 to 26 minutes or until toothpick inserted in center comes out clean. Remove brownies from oven; turn oven to broil. Meanwhile, in small bowl combine 2 tablespoons margarine, brown sugar, corn syrup and milk; blend well. Stir in coconut and pecans. Drop mixture by teaspoonfuls evenly over warm brownies; spread gently. Broil 4 inches from heat for 1 to 1½ minutes or until bubbly. Cool completely; cut into bars. 16 bars.

HIGH ALTITUDE – Above 3500 Feet: Increase flour to 1¼ cups. Bake as directed above.

NUTRITION INFORMATION

SERVING SIZE: 1 BAR		PERCENT U.S. RDA PER SERVING	
CALORIES	240	PROTEIN	4%
PROTEIN	3 g	VITAMIN A	6%
CARBOHYDRATE	28 g	VITAMIN C	*
FAT	14 g	THIAMINE	4%
CHOLESTEROL	27 mg	RIBOFLAVIN	4%
SODIUM	140 mg	NIACIN	2%
POTASSIUM	95 mg	CALCIUM	2%
		IRON	6%

* Contains less than 2% of the U.S. RDA of this nutrient.

German Chocolate Saucepan Brownies

BARS

Rely on bars for versatility and flavor.

What could be easier than spreading batter in a pan, then baking and cutting. Whether bars are frosted or unfrosted, fancy or plain, downright delicious describes them and they are great for many occasions. For potlucks or family get-togethers, cream-filled and crumb-topped **Date Maple Cream Bars** are perfect. Bars that are ideal for shipping to friends or relatives include chewy **Peanut Brittle Bars** and wholesome **Applesauce Granola Bars**. Special occasions for young and old will be brightened with **Party Funfetti®Bars**.

Pictured:
CHOCOLATY CARAMEL PECAN BARS
page 68

These indulgent candy-like bars won rave reviews from our taste panel of home economists. A buttery, tender crust is topped with caramel, pecans and chocolate. What could be more inviting?

CHOCOLATY CARAMEL PECAN BARS

(pictured on p. 66)

CRUST
½ cup powdered sugar
½ cup margarine or butter, softened
1 tablespoon whipping cream
1 cup Pillsbury's BEST® All Purpose or Unbleached Flour

FILLING
24 vanilla caramels, unwrapped
⅓ cup whipping cream
2 cups pecan halves

TOPPING
1 teaspoon margarine or butter
½ cup milk chocolate chips
2 tablespoons whipping cream

Heat oven to 325°F. Grease 9-inch square pan. In medium bowl, combine powdered sugar, ½ cup margarine and 1 tablespoon whipping cream; blend well. Lightly spoon flour into measuring cup; level off. Add flour; mix until crumbly. With floured hands, press evenly in greased pan. Bake at 325°F. for 15 to 20 minutes or until firm to touch.

Meanwhile, in medium saucepan combine caramels and ⅓ cup whipping cream. Cook over low heat until caramels are melted and mixture is smooth, stirring occasionally. Remove from heat. Add pecans; stir well to coat. Immediately spoon over baked crust; spread carefully to cover.

In small saucepan over low heat, melt 1 teaspoon margarine and chocolate chips, stirring constantly. Stir in 2 tablespoons whipping cream. Drizzle over filling. Refrigerate 1 hour or until filling is firm. Cut into bars. 24 bars.

NUTRITION INFORMATION

SERVING SIZE: 1 BAR		PERCENT U.S. RDA PER SERVING	
CALORIES	200	PROTEIN	2%
PROTEIN	2 g	VITAMIN A	4%
CARBOHYDRATE	18 g	VITAMIN C	*
FAT	14 g	THIAMINE	4%
CHOLESTEROL	8 mg	RIBOFLAVIN	4%
SODIUM	75 mg	NIACIN	2%
POTASSIUM	75 mg	CALCIUM	2%
		IRON	2%

* Contains less than 2% of the U.S. RDA of this nutrient.

These granola-like bars make a great snack or a quick on-the-run breakfast.

OATMEAL CRUNCH BARS

4 cups quick-cooking rolled oats
1½ cups chopped nuts
1 cup firmly packed brown sugar
1 cup coconut
1 teaspoon salt
¾ cup margarine or butter, melted
¾ cup orange marmalade

Heat oven to 400°F. Grease 15x10x1-inch baking pan. In large bowl, combine all ingredients; mix well. Press in greased pan.

Bake at 400°F. for 18 to 22 minutes or until golden brown. Cool completely; cut into bars. 48 bars.

NUTRITION INFORMATION

SERVING SIZE: 1 BAR		PERCENT U.S. RDA PER SERVING	
CALORIES	110	PROTEIN	2%
PROTEIN	2 g	VITAMIN A	2%
CARBOHYDRATE	14 g	VITAMIN C	*
FAT	6 g	THIAMINE	4%
CHOLESTEROL	0 mg	RIBOFLAVIN	*
SODIUM	80 mg	NIACIN	*
POTASSIUM	65 mg	CALCIUM	*
		IRON	2%

* Contains less than 2% of the U.S. RDA of this nutrient.

The natural sweetness of prunes eliminates the need for additional sugar in the filling mixture.

OATMEAL PRUNE BARS

FILLING
1¼ cups finely chopped dried
     pitted prunes
½ cup water
1 tablespoon lemon juice

BASE
1 cup quick-cooking rolled oats
⅔ cup Pillsbury's BEST® All
     Purpose or Unbleached
     Flour
½ cup firmly packed brown
     sugar
¼ teaspoon baking soda
¼ teaspoon salt
¼ teaspoon cinnamon
6 tablespoons margarine,
     melted

Grease 8-inch square pan. In medium saucepan, combine all filling ingredients. Cook over medium heat until thick, stirring frequently. Cool slightly.

Heat oven to 350°F. In medium bowl, combine all base ingredients except margarine; blend well. Stir in margarine until mixture is crumbly. Reserve ¾ cup of crumb mixture; press remaining mixture in bottom of greased pan. Spread filling over base; sprinkle with reserved crumb mixture, pressing down slightly.

Bake at 350°F. for 22 to 27 minutes or until light golden brown. Cool completely; cut into bars. 16 bars.

HIGH ALTITUDE – Above 3500 Feet: No change.

NUTRITION INFORMATION

SERVING SIZE: 1 BAR		PERCENT U.S. RDA PER SERVING	
CALORIES	130	PROTEIN	2%
PROTEIN	2 g	VITAMIN A	8%
CARBOHYDRATE	22 g	VITAMIN C	*
FAT	5 g	THIAMINE	6%
CHOLESTEROL	0 mg	RIBOFLAVIN	2%
SODIUM	105 mg	NIACIN	2%
POTASSIUM	140 mg	CALCIUM	*
		IRON	6%

* Contains less than 2% of the U.S. RDA of this nutrient.

Cook's Note

PACKING COOKIES, BROWNIES AND BARS FOR SHIPPING

Best choices:
- Unfrosted crispy or chewy bars
- Chewy or fudgy brownies
- Firm cut-out cookies
- Drop cookies

Poor choices:
- Cake-like brownies or bars
- Soft cookies
- Cookies or bars with soft frosting
- Cookies or bars with ingredients that might melt or spoil in warm weather

How to pack:
- Use plastic or metal containers
- Line containers with plastic wrap, waxed paper or aluminum foil
- Pack cookies, brownies or bars snugly
- Cushion cookies with crumpled waxed paper so they do not shift
- Wrap more tender cookies individually in plastic wrap or in back-to-back pairs

How to ship:
- Pack each container of cookies, brownies or bars in a strong cardboard shipping box
- Tuck crumpled newspaper or waxed paper around container to prevent shifting
- Label box carefully
- Mark the shipping box "perishable" to encourage careful handling

Serve these dessert bars with coffee or tea and garnish each serving with a sprinkling of lemon peel.

SUNNY LEMON CHEESECAKE SQUARES

1 pkg. Pillsbury Plus® Lemon
Cake Mix
½ cup margarine or butter,
softened
1 (8-oz.) pkg. cream cheese,
softened
1 (11-oz.) can mandarin orange
segments, well drained
2 eggs
⅔ cup coconut

Heat oven to 325°F. Lightly grease 9-inch square pan. Reserve 1 cup of the dry cake mix. In large bowl, combine remaining cake mix and margarine at low speed until crumbly. Reserve 1 cup of the crumb mixture. Press remaining crumb mixture in bottom of greased pan.

In same bowl, combine reserved 1 cup cake mix, cream cheese, orange segments and eggs at medium speed until well blended. Stir in coconut. Spread over base. Sprinkle with reserved 1 cup crumb mixture.

Bake at 325°F. for 30 to 40 minutes or until center is set. Cool completely. Refrigerate until set; cut into bars. Store in refrigerator. 16 bars.

HIGH ALTITUDE – Above 3500 Feet: No change.

NUTRITION INFORMATION

SERVING SIZE: 1 BAR		PERCENT U.S. RDA PER SERVING	
CALORIES	260	PROTEIN	4%
PROTEIN	3 g	VITAMIN A	10%
CARBOHYDRATE	29 g	VITAMIN C	4%
FAT	15 g	THIAMINE	6%
CHOLESTEROL	42 mg	RIBOFLAVIN	6%
SODIUM	310 mg	NIACIN	2%
POTASSIUM	70 mg	CALCIUM	6%
		IRON	4%

What a wonderful combination of flavors and texture in these easy-to-prepare bars. Your family will love them!

CHEWY CHOCOLATE CRUNCH BARS

BASE
1 pkg. Pillsbury Plus® Yellow
Cake Mix
⅓ cup coconut
½ cup margarine or butter,
softened
1 egg
1 cup crisp rice cereal

TOPPING
1 (12-oz.) pkg. (2 cups) semi-
sweet chocolate chips
2 cups miniature
marshmallows
1 can Pillsbury Coconut
Almond Frosting Supreme™
2 cups crisp rice cereal

Heat oven to 350°F. In large bowl, combine cake mix, coconut, margarine and egg until crumbly. Stir in 1 cup cereal. Press in bottom of ungreased 15x10x1-inch baking pan or 13x9-inch pan. Bake at 350°F. for 15 to 25 minutes or until light golden brown. Cool.

In large saucepan over low heat, melt chocolate chips, marshmallows and frosting, stirring constantly. Stir in 2 cups cereal. Spoon evenly over cooled base; carefully spread to cover. Cool completely; cut into bars. 48 bars.

HIGH ALTITUDE – Above 3500 Feet: No change.

NUTRITION INFORMATION

SERVING SIZE: 1 BAR		PERCENT U.S. RDA PER SERVING	
CALORIES	140	PROTEIN	*
PROTEIN	1 g	VITAMIN A	2%
CARBOHYDRATE	18 g	VITAMIN C	*
FAT	7 g	THIAMINE	2%
CHOLESTEROL	4 mg	RIBOFLAVIN	2%
SODIUM	130 mg	NIACIN	2%
POTASSIUM	35 mg	CALCIUM	2%
		IRON	2%

* Contains less than 2% of the U.S. RDA of this nutrient.

PEANUT CREAM BARS

BASE
2 cups Pillsbury's BEST® All Purpose or Unbleached Flour
⅔ cup firmly packed brown sugar
½ cup margarine or butter, softened
¼ cup creamy peanut butter
1 egg

FILLING
1 (8-oz.) pkg. cream cheese, softened
⅓ cup firmly packed brown sugar
½ teaspoon vanilla
2 tablespoons flour
2 eggs
1 cup peanut butter chips

GLAZE
1 oz. (1 square) semi-sweet chocolate
1 teaspoon oil

Heat oven to 350°F. Lightly spoon flour into measuring cup; level off. In large bowl, combine all base ingredients; mix well. Press mixture in ungreased 13x9-inch pan. Bake at 350°F. for 15 to 20 minutes or until light golden brown.

In small bowl, beat cream cheese, ⅓ cup brown sugar and vanilla until fluffy. Add 2 tablespoons flour and 2 eggs; blend well. Pour filling over partially baked base. Sprinkle peanut butter chips evenly over filling. Return to oven and bake an additional 15 to 20 minutes or until firm to the touch. Cool completely.

In small saucepan over low heat, melt chocolate and oil, stirring constantly. Drizzle over filling. Let stand until set. Cut into bars. Store in refrigerator. 36 bars.

TIP:
To soften cream cheese in microwave, unwrap it and place it in a small microwave-safe bowl. Microwave 8 oz. on MEDIUM for 1 to 1½ minutes.

HIGH ALTITUDE – Above 3500 Feet: No change.

NUTRITION INFORMATION

SERVING SIZE: 1 BAR		PERCENT U.S. RDA PER SERVING	
CALORIES	140	PROTEIN	4%
PROTEIN	3 g	VITAMIN A	4%
CARBOHYDRATE	15 g	VITAMIN C	*
FAT	8 g	THIAMINE	4%
CHOLESTEROL	25 mg	RIBOFLAVIN	4%
SODIUM	75 mg	NIACIN	4%
POTASSIUM	80 mg	CALCIUM	2%
		IRON	4%

* Contains less than 2% of the U.S. RDA of this nutrient.

A sprinkle of sunshine tops these easy bars made with cake mix.

SUNSHINE VANILLA BARS

(pictured on cover)

1 pkg. Pillsbury Plus® Sunshine Vanilla Cake Mix
½ cup margarine or butter, melted
2 eggs
½ cup chopped nuts, if desired
1 can Pillsbury Sunshine Vanilla Funfetti® Frosting

Heat oven to 375°F. Grease 15x10x1-inch baking pan. In large bowl, combine cake mix, margarine and eggs; stir by hand until thoroughly moistened. Stir in nuts. Spread in greased pan.

Bake at 375°F. for 13 to 17 minutes or until light golden brown and toothpick inserted in center comes out clean. Cool completely.

Frost cooled bars; sprinkle with candy bits from frosting. Cut into bars. 48 bars.

HIGH ALTITUDE – Above 3500 Feet: No change.

NUTRITION INFORMATION

SERVING SIZE: 1 BAR		PERCENT U.S. RDA PER SERVING	
CALORIES	110	PROTEIN	*
PROTEIN	1 g	VITAMIN A	*
CARBOHYDRATE	15 g	VITAMIN C	*
FAT	6 g	THIAMINE	2%
CHOLESTEROL	9 mg	RIBOFLAVIN	*
SODIUM	115 mg	NIACIN	*
POTASSIUM	15 mg	CALCIUM	2%
		IRON	*

* Contains less than 2% of the U.S. RDA of this nutrient.

RECIPE  MAKE-OVER

Light and Spicy Pumpkin Bars

We've redesigned this popular recipe to be lighter, healthier and just as tasty.

For family get-togethers, church functions or just packing in lunches, **Pumpkin Bars** are an all-time favorite. We've included the dense nut-and-raisin-studded version because we know its favorite flavor can't be beat. Our original recipe is topped with luscious cream cheese frosting, a trademark of these popular bars.

Light and Spicy Pumpkin Bars were developed for those who prefer a lighter bar. Eggs, oil and sugar are reduced, resulting in lower fat, cholesterol and calorie counts. Spices are deliciously delicate and pumpkin flavor is intensified. Though the frosting has been scaled down, it's just as creamy and delicious as the original. You'll love the tempting touch of yogurt.

Whether you choose the original version or the lighter version, we know you will be delighted!

Light and Spicy Pumpkin Bars

LIGHT AND SPICY PUMPKIN BARS

(pictured on left)

BARS
 1 cup Pillsbury's BEST® All Purpose or Unbleached Flour
 1 cup Pillsbury's BEST® Whole Wheat Flour
 1½ cups firmly packed brown sugar
 2 teaspoons baking powder
 1 teaspoon baking soda
 1 teaspoon cinnamon
 ½ teaspoon nutmeg
 ½ teaspoon cloves
 ¼ teaspoon salt
 ½ cup oil
 ½ cup apple juice
 1 (16-oz.) can (2 cups) pumpkin
 2 eggs

FROSTING
 1½ cups powdered sugar
 2 tablespoons margarine, softened
 ½ teaspoon vanilla
 2 to 3 tablespoons plain yogurt

Heat oven to 350°F. Grease and flour 15x10x1-inch baking pan. Lightly spoon flour into measuring cup; level off. In large bowl, beat all bar ingredients at low speed until moistened. Beat 2 minutes at medium speed. Spread in greased and floured pan.

Bake at 350°F. for 20 to 30 minutes or until toothpick inserted in center comes out clean. Cool completely.

In medium bowl, combine all frosting ingredients, adding enough yogurt for desired spreading consistency; beat until smooth. Frost cooled bars; sprinkle with nutmeg, if desired. Refrigerate to set frosting; cut into bars. 48 bars.

HIGH ALTITUDE - Above 3500 Feet: Increase all purpose flour to 1⅓ cups. Decrease baking powder to 1 teaspoon. Bake as directed above.

Nutrition Information on page 74

PUMPKIN BARS

BARS
 2 cups Pillsbury's BEST® All Purpose or Unbleached Flour
 2 cups sugar
 2 teaspoons baking powder
 1 teaspoon baking soda
 1 teaspoon cinnamon
 1 teaspoon nutmeg
 ½ teaspoon salt
 ½ teaspoon cloves
 1 cup oil
 1 (16-oz.) can (2 cups) pumpkin
 4 eggs
 ½ cup chopped nuts
 ½ cup raisins

FROSTING
 2 cups powdered sugar
 ⅓ cup margarine or butter, softened
 1 (3-oz.) pkg. cream cheese, softened
 1 tablespoon milk
 1 teaspoon vanilla

Heat oven to 350°F. Grease 15x10x1-inch baking pan. Lightly spoon flour into measuring cup; level off. In large bowl, combine all bar ingredients except nuts and raisins; beat at low speed until moistened. Beat 2 minutes at medium speed. Stir in nuts and raisins. Pour into greased pan.

Bake at 350°F. for 25 to 30 minutes or until toothpick inserted in center comes out clean. Cool completely.

In small bowl, combine all frosting ingredients; beat until smooth. Spread over cooled bars. Cut into bars. Store in refrigerator. 48 bars.

HIGH ALTITUDE - Above 3500 Feet: Decrease baking soda to ½ teaspoon. Bake at 375°F. for 30 to 35 minutes.

NUTRITION INFORMATION

SERVING SIZE: 1 BAR		PERCENT U.S. RDA PER SERVING	
CALORIES	150	PROTEIN	2%
PROTEIN	2 g	VITAMIN A	45%
CARBOHYDRATE	20 g	VITAMIN C	*
FAT	8 g	THIAMINE	2%
CHOLESTEROL	20 mg	RIBOFLAVIN	2%
SODIUM	85 mg	NIACIN	*
POTASSIUM	50 mg	CALCIUM	*
		IRON	2%

* Contains less than 2% of the U.S. RDA of this nutrient.

Baklava is a heavenly Greek pastry bar made from layers of phyllo dough, sweet spices, honey and nuts. We've simplified the traditional method by using refrigerated crescent roll dough for the pastry, and we've combined it with a delicious blend of filling ingredients.

EASY BAKLAVA BARS

CRUST
1 (8-oz.) can Pillsbury
  Refrigerated Quick Crescent
  Dinner Rolls
2 tablespoons butter or
  margarine, melted

FILLING
2 cups finely chopped walnuts
1 cup coconut
1 cup quick-cooking rolled oats
2 tablespoons brown sugar
½ cup butter or margarine,
  melted
½ teaspoon cinnamon
⅛ teaspoon allspice
⅛ teaspoon cloves

GLAZE
½ cup sugar
¼ cup water
¼ cup butter or margarine
2 tablespoons honey
1 tablespoon brandy, if desired
1 teaspoon lemon juice
¼ teaspoon cinnamon
3 whole cloves

Heat oven to 350°F. Grease 15x10x1-inch baking pan. Unroll dough into 2 long rectangles. Place in greased pan; press over bottom to form crust. Seal perforations. Brush with 2 tablespoons melted butter. Bake at 350°F. for 5 minutes. Remove from oven.

In large bowl, combine all filling ingredients; blend well. Spoon evenly over partially baked crust; gently press down. Return to oven and bake an additional 15 to 20 minutes or until golden brown.

In small saucepan, combine all glaze ingredients. Bring to a boil. Reduce heat; simmer 2 to 3 minutes, stirring constantly. Remove whole cloves. Drizzle glaze evenly over warm bars. Cool completely; cut into bars. 48 bars.

NUTRITION INFORMATION

SERVING SIZE: 1 BAR		PERCENT U.S. RDA PER SERVING	
CALORIES	110	PROTEIN	2%
PROTEIN	1 g	VITAMIN A	2%
CARBOHYDRATE	8 g	VITAMIN C	*
FAT	8 g	THIAMINE	2%
CHOLESTEROL	10 mg	RIBOFLAVIN	*
SODIUM	75 mg	NIACIN	*
POTASSIUM	50 mg	CALCIUM	*
		IRON	2%

* Contains less than 2% of the U.S. RDA of this nutrient.

Light and Spicy Pumpkin Bars
Continued from page 73

NUTRITION INFORMATION

SERVING SIZE: 1 BAR		PERCENT U.S. RDA PER SERVING	
CALORIES	90	PROTEIN	*
PROTEIN	1 g	VITAMIN A	40%
CARBOHYDRATE	15 g	VITAMIN C	*
FAT	3 g	THIAMINE	2%
CHOLESTEROL	9 mg	RIBOFLAVIN	2%
SODIUM	60 mg	NIACIN	*
POTASSIUM	65 mg	CALCIUM	2%
		IRON	2%

* Contains less than 2% of the U.S. RDA of this nutrient.

Raisins, dates and prunes plus a subtle coffee flavor make these bars especially pleasing. Serve them sprinkled with powdered sugar or cut them into squares and top with whipped cream.

SWEDISH FRUIT BARS

FILLING
- 1 cup raisins
- 1 cup chopped dates
- 1 cup chopped pitted prunes
- ¾ cup firmly packed brown sugar
- 1 cup coffee
- 2 tablespoons lemon juice

BARS
- 1 cup chopped walnuts or pecans
- 2¼ cups Pillsbury's BEST® All Purpose or Unbleached Flour
- 1 cup sugar
- ½ cup firmly packed brown sugar
- ¾ cup margarine or butter, softened
- ½ teaspoon salt
- ½ teaspoon baking soda
- ¾ teaspoon cinnamon
- ¼ teaspoon nutmeg
- 1 cup buttermilk*
- 1 egg
- 1 tablespoon powdered sugar, if desired

In medium saucepan, combine all filling ingredients except lemon juice. Cook over medium heat until thickened, stirring occasionally. Remove from heat; stir in lemon juice. Cool slightly.

Heat oven to 350°F. Sprinkle walnuts evenly over bottom of ungreased 13x9-inch pan. Lightly spoon flour into measuring cup; level off. In large bowl, combine 2 cups of the flour, ½ cup of the sugar, brown sugar and margarine at low speed until crumbly. Sprinkle 2 cups of the crumb mixture over walnuts; press firmly. Carefully spread cooled filling evenly over crumb base. Add remaining ¼ cup flour, ½ cup sugar, salt, baking soda, cinnamon, nutmeg, buttermilk and egg to remaining crumb mixture; beat well. Carefully pour batter over filling.

Bake at 350°F. for 30 to 40 minutes or until top springs back when touched lightly in center. Cool completely. Sprinkle with powdered sugar. Cut into bars. 36 bars.

TIP:
* To substitute for buttermilk, use 1 tablespoon vinegar or lemon juice plus milk to make 1 cup.

HIGH ALTITUDE - Above 3500 Feet: No change.

NUTRITION INFORMATION

SERVING SIZE: 1 BAR		PERCENT U.S. RDA PER SERVING	
CALORIES	180	PROTEIN	2%
PROTEIN	2 g	VITAMIN A	4%
CARBOHYDRATE	30 g	VITAMIN C	*
FAT	6 g	THIAMINE	6%
CHOLESTEROL	6 mg	RIBOFLAVIN	4%
SODIUM	100 mg	NIACIN	4%
POTASSIUM	170 mg	CALCIUM	2%
		IRON	6%

* Contains less than 2% of the U.S. RDA of this nutrient.

Cooking the filling for this luscious bar softens the dates and thickens the mixture. These bars have delicious old-fashioned flavor and will remind you of the date bars that your grandma used to make.

DATE MAPLE CREAM BARS

(pictured on right)

FILLING
¾ **cup firmly packed brown sugar**
1 **tablespoon cornstarch**
1½ **cups finely chopped dates**
1½ **cups dairy sour cream**
1 **teaspoon maple extract**
3 **egg yolks**

BASE AND TOPPING
1¼ **cups Pillsbury's BEST® All Purpose or Unbleached Flour**
2 **cups quick-cooking rolled oats**
¾ **cup firmly packed brown sugar**
½ **teaspoon baking soda**
¾ **cup margarine or butter**

Heat oven to 350°F. Grease 13x9-inch pan. In medium saucepan, combine all filling ingredients. Cook over medium heat until slightly thickened, stirring constantly. Cool slightly.

Lightly spoon flour into measuring cup; level off. In medium bowl, combine flour, rolled oats, ¾ cup brown sugar and baking soda; mix well. With pastry blender or fork, cut in margarine until mixture is crumbly. Reserve 1½ cups oat mixture for topping. Press remaining oat mixture evenly in bottom of greased pan.

Bake at 350°F. for 10 minutes. Spoon filling evenly over base. Sprinkle with reserved oat mixture. Return to oven and bake an additional 20 to 30 minutes or until light golden brown and set. Cool completely; cut into bars. 36 bars.

HIGH ALTITUDE – Above 3500 Feet: No change.

NUTRITION INFORMATION

SERVING SIZE: 1 BAR		PERCENT U.S. RDA PER SERVING	
CALORIES	150	PROTEIN	2%
PROTEIN	2 g	VITAMIN A	4%
CARBOHYDRATE	21 g	VITAMIN C	*
FAT	7 g	THIAMINE	4%
CHOLESTEROL	23 mg	RIBOFLAVIN	2%
SODIUM	70 mg	NIACIN	2%
POTASSIUM	120 mg	CALCIUM	2%
		IRON	4%

* Contains less than 2% of the U.S. RDA of this nutrient.

Cook's Note

DATES

Dates are oval, glossy, thin-skinned fruits that can range from golden to dark mahogany in color. They grow on date palm trees in California, Arizona and the Middle East.

Fresh dates can be found in large supermarkets and specialty markets from late summer through the winter, with peak supplies in November. Dried dates are available year-round. You'll find them whole (pitted and unpitted) or chopped. Fresh and dried dates are interchangeable in most recipes.

Fresh dates should be refrigerated and used within two weeks. Dried dates can be stored, airtight, at room temperature in a cool, dry place for up to six months, or in the refrigerator for up to a year.

Date Maple Cream Bars

Maraschino cherries are packed in a concentrated sugar syrup, which is usually lightly flavored with almond. You'll enjoy their sweet, distinctive flavor in these pretty special-occasion bars.

CHERRY WALNUT BARS

CRUST
2 cups Pillsbury's BEST® All Purpose or Unbleached Flour
½ cup sugar
1 cup margarine or butter, softened

FILLING
2 eggs, slightly beaten
1½ cups firmly packed brown sugar
¼ cup flour
½ teaspoon baking powder
½ teaspoon salt
½ cup chopped maraschino cherries, drained, reserving liquid
1 cup chopped walnuts

GLAZE
1½ cups powdered sugar
3 to 4 tablespoons reserved maraschino cherry liquid

Heat oven to 350°F. Grease 13x9-inch pan. Lightly spoon flour into measuring cup; level off. In large bowl, combine all crust ingredients; mix until crumbly. Press crumb mixture in greased pan. Bake at 350°F. for 18 to 22 minutes or until light golden brown.

In small bowl, beat eggs and brown sugar until fluffy. Add ¼ cup flour, baking powder and salt; mix well. Stir in cherries and walnuts; pour filling over partially baked crust. Return to oven and bake an additional 25 to 30 minutes or until golden brown and filling is set. Cool completely.

In small bowl, combine glaze ingredients, adding enough cherry liquid for desired spreading consistency; blend until smooth. Spread evenly over cooled bars. Let stand until set; cut into bars. 36 bars.

HIGH ALTITUDE – Above 3500 Feet: No change.

NUTRITION INFORMATION

SERVING SIZE: 1 BAR		PERCENT U.S. RDA PER SERVING	
CALORIES	170	PROTEIN	2%
PROTEIN	2 g	VITAMIN A	4%
CARBOHYDRATE	24 g	VITAMIN C	*
FAT	7 g	THIAMINE	4%
CHOLESTEROL	12 mg	RIBOFLAVIN	2%
SODIUM	100 mg	NIACIN	2%
POTASSIUM	65 mg	CALCIUM	*
		IRON	4%

* Contains less than 2% of the U.S. RDA of this nutrient.

Using the larger amount of chocolate chips will result in a slightly chewier, more chocolaty bar.

CHOCOLATE CREAM BARS

CRUST
2½ cups Pillsbury's BEST® All Purpose or Unbleached Flour
2 cups rolled oats
1½ cups firmly packed brown sugar
1 teaspoon baking soda
½ teaspoon salt
1 cup margarine or butter, softened

FILLING
1 to 2 cups (6 or 12-oz. pkg.) semi-sweet chocolate chips
1 (14-oz.) can sweetened condensed milk (not evaporated)
2 tablespoons margarine or butter
2 teaspoons vanilla
1 cup chopped nuts

Heat oven to 350°F. Lightly spoon flour into measuring cup; level off. In large bowl, combine all crust ingredients; mix at low speed until crumbly. Press 4 cups crumb mixture in ungreased 15x10x1-inch baking pan (reserve remaining crumb mixture for topping).

In medium saucepan, combine chocolate chips, condensed milk and 2 tablespoons margarine. Cook over low heat, stirring constantly until chocolate is melted and mixture is smooth. Stir in vanilla and nuts. Pour filling over crust; sprinkle with reserved crumb mixture.

Bake at 350°F. for 25 to 30 minutes or until golden brown. Cool completely; cut into bars. 48 bars.

HIGH ALTITUDE – Above 3500 Feet: No change.

NUTRITION INFORMATION

SERVING SIZE: 1 BAR		PERCENT U.S. RDA PER SERVING	
CALORIES	190	PROTEIN	4%
PROTEIN	3 g	VITAMIN A	4%
CARBOHYDRATE	24 g	VITAMIN C	*
FAT	10 g	THIAMINE	6%
CHOLESTEROL	4 mg	RIBOFLAVIN	6%
SODIUM	115 mg	NIACIN	2%
POTASSIUM	120 mg	CALCIUM	4%
		IRON	4%

* Contains less than 2% of the U.S. RDA of this nutrient.

Fudge marble cake mix makes it easy to create this two-layer bar, which features a chewy chocolate bottom.

BLACK BOTTOM ORANGE BARS

1 pkg. Pillsbury Plus® Fudge Marble or Fudge Swirl Cake Mix
¾ cup orange juice
¼ cup oil
2 eggs
½ cup coconut
1 to 2 teaspoons orange extract
½ cup semi-sweet chocolate chips
Powdered sugar

Heat oven to 350°F. Grease and flour 13x9-inch pan. Reserve marble pouch. In large bowl, combine cake mix, orange juice, oil and eggs at low speed until moistened; beat 2 minutes at high speed. Pour half of batter into a second bowl; stir in coconut and orange extract. To batter in first bowl, add reserved marble pouch and chocolate chips; mix well. Spread chocolate batter in greased and floured pan. Spoon coconut-orange batter evenly over chocolate batter; carefully spread to cover.

Bake at 350°F. for 25 to 35 minutes or until toothpick inserted in center comes out clean. Cool 30 minutes. Sprinkle with powdered sugar. Cool completely; cut into bars. 24 bars.

HIGH ALTITUDE – Above 3500 Feet: Add 3 tablespoons flour to dry cake mix. Bake at 375°F. for 25 to 35 minutes.

NUTRITION INFORMATION

SERVING SIZE: 1 BAR		PERCENT U.S. RDA PER SERVING	
CALORIES	150	PROTEIN	2%
PROTEIN	2 g	VITAMIN A	*
CARBOHYDRATE	22 g	VITAMIN C	2%
FAT	7 g	THIAMINE	2%
CHOLESTEROL	18 mg	RIBOFLAVIN	2%
SODIUM	150 mg	NIACIN	2%
POTASSIUM	55 mg	CALCIUM	2%
		IRON	2%

* Contains less than 2% of the U.S. RDA of this nutrient.

Deliciously chock full of raisins and orange flavor, these rich bars are great served with coffee or tea.

ORANGE RAISIN CRESCENT BARS

(pictured on right)

1 (8-oz.) can Pillsbury
    Refrigerated Quick Crescent
    Dinner Rolls
1 cup raisins
1 cup golden raisins
½ cup chopped walnuts or
    pecans
1 tablespoon grated orange peel
1 (14-oz.) can sweetened
    condensed milk (not
    evaporated)

Heat oven to 375°F. Unroll dough into 2 long rectangles. Place in ungreased 13x9-inch pan; press over bottom and ½ inch up sides to form crust. Seal perforations. Bake at 375°F. for 5 minutes.

In medium bowl, combine remaining ingredients; blend well. Spoon over partially baked crust to within ½ inch of edge. Return to oven and bake an additional 15 to 28 minutes or until edges of crust are golden brown. Cool completely; cut into bars. 36 bars.

NUTRITION INFORMATION

SERVING SIZE: 1 BAR		PERCENT U.S. RDA PER SERVING	
CALORIES	100	PROTEIN	2%
PROTEIN	2 g	VITAMIN A	*
CARBOHYDRATE	17 g	VITAMIN C	*
FAT	4 g	THIAMINE	2%
CHOLESTEROL	6 mg	RIBOFLAVIN	4%
SODIUM	70 mg	NIACIN	*
POTASSIUM	140 mg	CALCIUM	4%
		IRON	2%

* Contains less than 2% of the U.S. RDA of this nutrient.

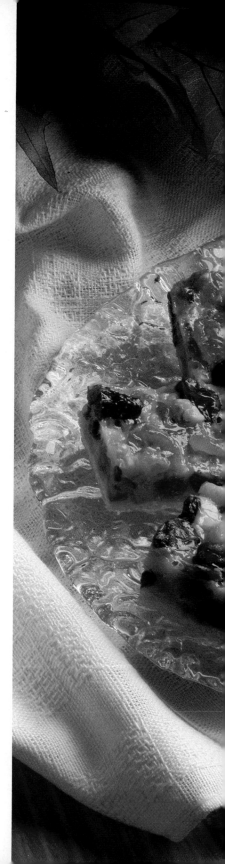

Orange Raisin Crescent Bars

Originally used to describe a strong, bitter-tasting coffee, "mocha" now refers to a sweet combination of coffee and chocolate. We've added almonds and almond flavoring to the mocha, creating an incredibly rich and indulgent dessert bar that's worthy of any chocolate craving!

MOCHA ALMOND FUDGE BARS

BARS
½ cup unsweetened cocoa
1 tablespoon instant coffee granules or crystals
1 cup margarine or butter
1 cup water
2 cups Pillsbury's BEST® All Purpose or Unbleached Flour
1 cup sugar
1 cup firmly packed brown sugar
1 teaspoon baking soda
½ cup buttermilk*
½ teaspoon almond extract
2 eggs
1 cup chopped almonds

GLAZE
1 tablespoon unsweetened cocoa
½ teaspoon instant coffee granules or crystals
1 tablespoon margarine or butter, melted
¼ teaspoon almond extract
1 cup powdered sugar
1 to 3 tablespoons milk

Heat oven to 375°F. Grease 15x10x1-inch baking pan. In medium saucepan, combine ½ cup cocoa, 1 tablespoon instant coffee, 1 cup margarine and water. Bring to a boil over medium-high heat, stirring occasionally; remove from heat. Cool 10 minutes. Lightly spoon flour into measuring cup; level off. In large bowl, combine flour, sugar, brown sugar, baking soda, buttermilk, ½ teaspoon almond extract and eggs. Add cocoa mixture to flour mixture. Beat until blended. Stir in almonds. Pour batter into greased pan.

Bake at 375°F. for 15 to 20 minutes or until toothpick inserted in center comes out clean. Cool completely.

In medium bowl, combine 1 tablespoon cocoa, ½ teaspoon instant coffee and 1 tablespoon margarine; blend until smooth. Stir in ¼ teaspoon almond extract, powdered sugar and enough milk for desired drizzling consistency; drizzle over cooled bars. Let stand until set. Cut into bars. 48 bars.

TIP:
* To substitute for buttermilk, use 1½ teaspoons vinegar or lemon juice plus milk to make ½ cup.

HIGH ALTITUDE – Above 3500 Feet: Decrease white sugar to ½ cup. Increase flour to 2½ cups. Bake as directed above.

NUTRITION INFORMATION

SERVING SIZE: 1 BAR		PERCENT U.S. RDA PER SERVING	
CALORIES	120	PROTEIN	2%
PROTEIN	2 g	VITAMIN A	2%
CARBOHYDRATE	16 g	VITAMIN C	*
FAT	6 g	THIAMINE	2%
CHOLESTEROL	9 mg	RIBOFLAVIN	4%
SODIUM	85 mg	NIACIN	2%
POTASSIUM	60 mg	CALCIUM	*
		IRON	2%

* Contains less than 2% of the U.S. RDA of this nutrient.

We love these deliciously rich bars.

SWEET DREAM BARS

BASE

 1 cup Pillsbury's BEST® All
   Purpose or Unbleached
   Flour
 ¼ cup sugar
 ½ cup margarine or butter

FILLING

 1 cup (13 squares) graham
   cracker crumbs
 ½ cup semi-sweet chocolate
   chips
 ½ cup chopped nuts
 1 teaspoon baking powder
 ¼ teaspoon salt
 1 (14-oz.) can sweetened
   condensed milk (not
   evaporated)

FROSTING

 1½ cups powdered sugar
 ½ cup margarine or butter,
   softened
 1 teaspoon vanilla

Heat oven to 350°F. Lightly spoon
flour into measuring cup; level off. In
small bowl, combine flour and sugar.
Using pastry blender or fork, cut in
½ cup margarine until crumbly. Press
in bottom of ungreased 13x9-inch
pan. Bake at 350°F. for 10 minutes.
Cool 10 minutes.

In large bowl, combine all filling
ingredients; blend well. Spoon evenly
over partially baked base. Return to
oven and bake an additional 15 to
20 minutes or until golden brown.
Cool completely.

In small bowl, blend all frosting
ingredients until smooth. Frost
cooled bars. Cut into bars. 36 bars.

HIGH ALTITUDE – Above 3500 Feet:
No change.

NUTRITION INFORMATION

SERVING SIZE: 1 BAR		PERCENT U.S. RDA PER SERVING	
CALORIES	160	PROTEIN	2%
PROTEIN	2 g	VITAMIN A	4%
CARBOHYDRATE	21 g	VITAMIN C	*
FAT	8 g	THIAMINE	2%
CHOLESTEROL	5 mg	RIBOFLAVIN	6%
SODIUM	115 mg	NIACIN	*
POTASSIUM	85 mg	CALCIUM	4%
		IRON	2%

* Contains less than 2% of the U.S. RDA of this nutrient.

Store these bars in the refrigerator.

TOFFEE CREAM BARS

BASE

 1 cup Pillsbury's BEST® All
   Purpose or Unbleached
   Flour
 ½ cup sugar
 ½ cup margarine or butter
 ¼ teaspoon salt

FILLING

 1 can Pillsbury Coconut Pecan
   Frosting Supreme™
 1 (3-oz.) pkg. cream cheese,
   softened
 1 egg

GLAZE

 ⅓ cup semi-sweet chocolate
   chips
 2 teaspoons shortening

Heat oven to 350°F. In small bowl,
combine all base ingredients. Beat at
medium speed until crumbly. Press
mixture in ungreased 13x9-inch pan.
Bake at 350°F. for 17 to 22 minutes or
until light golden brown.

In small bowl, combine all filling
ingredients at medium speed until
blended. Spread filling over partially
baked base. Return to oven and bake
an additional 22 to 32 minutes or
until golden brown and center is
almost set. Cool completely.

Melt glaze ingredients in small
saucepan over low heat, stirring
constantly until smooth. Drizzle over
cooled bars. Refrigerate at least
1 hour. Cut into bars. Store in
refrigerator. 36 bars.

HIGH ALTITUDE – Above 3500 Feet:
No change.

NUTRITION INFORMATION

SERVING SIZE: 1 BAR		PERCENT U.S. RDA PER SERVING	
CALORIES	120	PROTEIN	*
PROTEIN	1 g	VITAMIN A	2%
CARBOHYDRATE	12 g	VITAMIN C	*
FAT	8 g	THIAMINE	2%
CHOLESTEROL	8 mg	RIBOFLAVIN	*
SODIUM	75 mg	NIACIN	*
POTASSIUM	30 mg	CALCIUM	*
		IRON	*

* Contains less than 2% of the U.S. RDA of this nutrient.

We've given you two choices of cereal to make these snack squares. Use fresh marshmallows that will melt completely to ensure a soft and chewy bar. Store these bars tightly covered at room temperature.

SWEET AND CRUNCHY CEREAL SQUARES

(pictured on right)

1 cup peanut butter
⅓ cup honey
¼ cup margarine or butter
1 (10½-oz.) pkg. marshmallows
6 cups crispy honey graham cereal squares or corn cereal squares
1 cup candy corn

Grease 13x9-inch pan. In 4-quart saucepan or Dutch oven, combine peanut butter, honey, margarine and marshmallows. Cook over low heat until marshmallows are melted, stirring occasionally. Carefully stir in cereal and candy corn. Using wet or greased spatula, spread in greased pan. Cool completely; cut into bars. 36 bars.

NUTRITION INFORMATION

SERVING SIZE: 1 BAR		PERCENT U.S. RDA PER SERVING	
CALORIES	130	PROTEIN	2%
PROTEIN	2 g	VITAMIN A	6%
CARBOHYDRATE	21 g	VITAMIN C	6%
FAT	5 g	THIAMINE	6%
CHOLESTEROL	0 mg	RIBOFLAVIN	6%
SODIUM	130 mg	NIACIN	10%
POTASSIUM	70 mg	CALCIUM	*
		IRON	8%

* Contains less than 2% of the U.S. RDA of this nutrient.

These bars are especially appropriate for a child's party or special occasion. Kids will delight in the rainbow of colors!

PARTY FUNFETTI® BARS

(pictured on right)

1 pkg. Pillsbury Plus® Funfetti Cake Mix
½ cup margarine or butter, melted
2 eggs
½ cup chopped nuts, if desired
1 can Pillsbury Chocolate Funfetti® Frosting

Heat oven to 375°F. Grease 15x10x1-inch baking pan. In large bowl, combine cake mix, margarine and eggs; stir by hand until thoroughly moistened. Stir in candy bits from cake mix and nuts. Spread in greased pan.

Bake at 375°F. for 13 to 17 minutes or until light golden brown and toothpick inserted in center comes out clean. Cool completely.

Frost cooled bars; sprinkle with candy bits from frosting. Cut into bars. 48 bars.

HIGH ALTITUDE – Above 3500 Feet: No change.

NUTRITION INFORMATION

SERVING SIZE: 1 BAR		PERCENT U.S. RDA PER SERVING	
CALORIES	110	PROTEIN	*
PROTEIN	1 g	VITAMIN A	*
CARBOHYDRATE	15 g	VITAMIN C	*
FAT	5 g	THIAMINE	2%
CHOLESTEROL	9 mg	RIBOFLAVIN	*
SODIUM	110 mg	NIACIN	*
POTASSIUM	45 mg	CALCIUM	2%
		IRON	*

* Contains less than 2% of the U.S. RDA of this nutrient.

Party Funfetti® Bars
Sweet And Crunchy Cereal Squares

There's whole grain goodness in each and every one of these delicious bars. They are a great after-school snack or lunch box addition.

APPLESAUCE GRANOLA BARS

½ cup firmly packed brown sugar
½ cup margarine or butter, softened
½ cup applesauce
2 teaspoons grated lemon peel
1 egg
1 cup Pillsbury's BEST® Whole Wheat Flour
¾ teaspoon baking soda
¼ teaspoon salt
¼ teaspoon allspice
1 cup granola
  Powdered sugar

Heat oven to 350°F. Grease 9-inch square pan. In large bowl, beat brown sugar and margarine until light and fluffy. Add applesauce, lemon peel and egg; blend well. Lightly spoon flour into measuring cup; level off. Add whole wheat flour, baking soda, salt and allspice; mix well. Stir in granola. Spread in greased pan.

Bake at 350°F. for 20 to 35 minutes or until toothpick inserted in center comes out clean. Cool completely. Sprinkle with powdered sugar. Cut into bars. 16 bars.

HIGH ALTITUDE – Above 3500 Feet: Decrease brown sugar to ⅓ cup. Bake as directed above.

NUTRITION INFORMATION

SERVING SIZE: 1 BAR		PERCENT U.S. RDA PER SERVING	
CALORIES	150	PROTEIN	4%
PROTEIN	2 g	VITAMIN A	4%
CARBOHYDRATE	18 g	VITAMIN C	*
FAT	8 g	THIAMINE	4%
CHOLESTEROL	13 mg	RIBOFLAVIN	2%
SODIUM	150 mg	NIACIN	2%
POTASSIUM	105 mg	CALCIUM	*
		IRON	4%

* Contains less than 2% of the U.S. RDA of this nutrient.

Easy-to-make dark chocolate bars are topped with creamy white chocolate. You'll find the combination irresistible.

DOUBLE CHOCOLATE FINGER BARS

BARS
1 pkg. Pillsbury Plus® Butter Recipe Chocolate Cake Mix
½ cup margarine or butter
1 (3-oz.) pkg. cream cheese
1 egg

FROSTING
1½ cups vanilla milk chips
¾ cup margarine or butter, softened
½ cup powdered sugar
  Chocolate sprinkles

Heat oven to 375°F. Place cake mix in large bowl. Using pastry blender or fork, cut in margarine and cream cheese until crumbly. Add egg; beat until dough is formed. Press dough evenly in ungreased 15x10x1-inch baking pan. Bake at 375°F. for 12 to 17 minutes or until set. Cool completely.

Melt vanilla milk chips in small saucepan over low heat, stirring constantly. Cool slightly. In small bowl, beat ¾ cup margarine and powdered sugar until fluffy. Gradually beat in cooled vanilla milk chips. Frost cooled bars; sprinkle with chocolate sprinkles. Cut pan of bars crosswise into 6 rows; cut lengthwise into 10 rows, forming finger-shaped bars. 60 bars.

HIGH ALTITUDE – Above 3500 Feet: No change.

NUTRITION INFORMATION

SERVING SIZE: 1 BAR		PERCENT U.S. RDA PER SERVING	
CALORIES	100	PROTEIN	*
PROTEIN	1 g	VITAMIN A	2%
CARBOHYDRATE	11 g	VITAMIN C	*
FAT	7 g	THIAMINE	*
CHOLESTEROL	6 mg	RIBOFLAVIN	2%
SODIUM	120 mg	NIACIN	*
POTASSIUM	60 mg	CALCIUM	2%
		IRON	*

* Contains less than 2% of the U.S. RDA of this nutrient.

Enjoy these not-too-sweet bars with hot apple cider on a crisp autumn day. Store them tightly covered.

GINGERBREAD BARS

½ cup sugar
½ cup oil
½ cup molasses
1 egg
1½ cups Pillsbury's BEST® All
    Purpose or Unbleached
    Flour
¾ teaspoon baking soda
½ teaspoon cinnamon
¼ teaspoon salt
¼ teaspoon nutmeg
¼ teaspoon cloves
¼ cup boiling water
½ cup granola
½ cup raisins
    Powdered sugar, if desired

Heat oven to 350°F. Grease 13x9-inch pan. In large bowl, beat sugar, oil and molasses until well blended. Add egg; blend well. Lightly spoon flour into measuring cup; level off. Add flour, baking soda, cinnamon, salt, nutmeg and cloves; mix well. Add boiling water; blend well. Stir in granola and raisins. Spread in greased pan.

Bake at 350°F. for 20 to 30 minutes or until toothpick inserted in center comes out clean. Cool completely. Sprinkle with powdered sugar. Cut into bars. 36 bars.

HIGH ALTITUDE – Above 3500 Feet: Increase flour to 2 cups. Increase boiling water to ½ cup. Bake as directed above.

NUTRITION INFORMATION

SERVING SIZE: 1 BAR		PERCENT U.S. RDA PER SERVING	
CALORIES	80	PROTEIN	*
PROTEIN	1 g	VITAMIN A	*
CARBOHYDRATE	12 g	VITAMIN C	*
FAT	4 g	THIAMINE	4%
CHOLESTEROL	6 mg	RIBOFLAVIN	2%
SODIUM	45 mg	NIACIN	2%
POTASSIUM	80 mg	CALCIUM	*
		IRON	4%

* Contains less than 2% of the U.S. RDA of this nutrient.

Cook's Note

MOLASSES

Often considered a healthful alternative to other sugars, molasses adds a distinctive flavor to any recipe. Molasses is a byproduct of the sugar refining process. **Light** molasses, lightest in both color and flavor, comes from the first boiling of the sugar syrup. **Dark** molasses comes from the second boiling; it is less sweet and is thicker and darker in color. **Blackstrap** molasses comes from the final boiling and is bitter in flavor.

Molasses is either sulphured or unsulphured, depending on whether sulphur was used in processing. In general, unsulphured molasses is lighter and has a cleaner sugar-cane flavor.

Light molasses is often used as pancake syrup. Dark molasses with its richer flavor is used in foods such as gingerbread and baked beans. Blackstrap molasses is not used much in cooking because of its bitter flavor. Because many health-conscious individuals feel blackstrap molasses has superior nutritional value (though this has not been proven), it is available in health food stores.

Molasses should be stored at room temperature in a cool, dark place. It will keep well for up to 12 months.

You'll enjoy the contrast between salty and sweet in these easy-to-make bars. The surprise is the nut-like flavor the whole wheat flour contributes to the crust.

PEANUT BRITTLE BARS

(pictured on right)

BASE
1½ cups Pillsbury's BEST® All Purpose or Unbleached Flour
½ cup Pillsbury's BEST® Whole Wheat Flour
1 cup firmly packed brown sugar
1 teaspoon baking soda
¼ teaspoon salt
1 cup margarine or butter

TOPPING
2 cups salted peanuts
1 cup milk chocolate chips
1 (12.5-oz.) jar caramel ice cream topping
3 tablespoons flour

Heat oven to 350°F. Grease 15x10x1-inch baking pan. Lightly spoon flour into measuring cup; level off. In large bowl, combine all base ingredients except margarine; mix well. Using pastry blender or fork, cut in margarine until crumbly. Press evenly in greased pan.

Bake at 350°F. for 8 to 14 minutes or until golden brown. Sprinkle peanuts and chocolate chips over warm base. In small bowl, combine caramel topping and 3 tablespoons flour; blend well. Drizzle evenly over chocolate chips and peanuts. Return to oven and bake an additional 12 to 18 minutes or until topping is set and golden brown. Cool completely; cut into bars. 48 bars.

HIGH ALTITUDE – Above 3500 Feet: No change.

NUTRITION INFORMATION

SERVING SIZE: 1 BAR		PERCENT U.S. RDA PER SERVING	
CALORIES	150	PROTEIN	4%
PROTEIN	3 g	VITAMIN A	2%
CARBOHYDRATE	17 g	VITAMIN C	*
FAT	8 g	THIAMINE	4%
CHOLESTEROL	1 mg	RIBOFLAVIN	2%
SODIUM	150 mg	NIACIN	6%
POTASSIUM	80 mg	CALCIUM	*
		IRON	2%

* Contains less than 2% of the U.S. RDA of this nutrient.

These quick-to-make cookie-bars are flavored with ready-to-spread frosting

PEANUT BUTTER SHORTBREAD

1 can Pillsbury Vanilla or Cream Cheese Frosting Supreme™
1½ cups peanut butter
¼ cup flour
1 egg
1½ cups chopped nuts

Heat oven to 325°F. Grease and flour 15x10x1-inch baking pan. In large bowl, combine 1 cup of the frosting, peanut butter, flour and egg at low speed until blended. Stir in nuts. Press in bottom of greased pan.

Bake at 325°F. for 15 to 20 minutes or until light golden brown. Spread remaining frosting on warm bars. Cool completely; cut into bars. 48 bars.

HIGH ALTITUDE – Above 3500 Feet: No change.

NUTRITION INFORMATION

SERVING SIZE: 1 BAR		PERCENT U.S. RDA PER SERVING	
CALORIES	120	PROTEIN	4%
PROTEIN	3 g	VITAMIN A	*
CARBOHYDRATE	10 g	VITAMIN C	*
FAT	8 g	THIAMINE	2%
CHOLESTEROL	5 mg	RIBOFLAVIN	*
SODIUM	55 mg	NIACIN	6%
POTASSIUM	85 mg	CALCIUM	*
		IRON	*

* Contains less than 2% of the U.S. RDA of this nutrient.

Peanut Brittle Bars

INDEX

MW = MICROWAVE DIRECTIONS, MWO = MICROWAVE DIRECTIONS ONLY

COOK'S NOTES

D

E

F

FROSTINGS

G

L

M

O

P

MW = MICROWAVE DIRECTIONS, MWO = MICROWAVE DIRECTIONS ONLY

R

S

T

W

Pumpkin Patch Brownies p. 56
Chocolate Cookie Mice p. 2?

Nutrition Information

Nutrition Information: Pillsbury recipe analysis is provided per serving or per unit of food and is based on the most current nutritional values available from the United States Department of Agriculture (USDA) and food manufacturers. Each recipe is calculated for number of calories; grams of protein, carbohydrate and fat; and milligrams of cholesterol, sodium and potassium.

Vitamin and mineral levels are stated as percentages of United States Recommended Daily Allowances. RDAs are the dietary standards determined by the U.S. Food and Drug Administration for healthy people. If you are following a medically prescribed diet, consult your physician or registered dietitian about using this nutrition information.

Calculating Nutrition Information: Recipe analysis is calculated on:

• A single serving based on the largest number of servings, or on a specific amount (1 tablespoon) or unit (1 cookie).

• The first ingredient or amount when more than one is listed.

• "If desired" or garnishing ingredients when they are included in the ingredient listing.

• Only the amount of a marinade or frying oil absorbed during preparation.

Using Nutrition Information: The amount of nutrients a person needs is determined by one's age, size and activity level. The following are general guidelines you can use for evaluating your daily food intake:

  Calories: 2350
  Protein: 45 to 65 grams
  Carbohydrates: 340 grams
  Fat: 80 grams or less
  Cholesterol: 300 milligrams or less
  Sodium: 2400 milligrams.

A nutritionally balanced diet recommends limiting intake of fat to 30% or less of total daily calories. One gram of fat is 9 calories. You can determine the fat content of recipes or products with the following formula:

$$\frac{\text{GRAMS OF FAT PER SERVING} \times 9}{\text{TOTAL CALORIES PER SERVING}} = \begin{array}{l}\text{PERCENT}\\ \text{OF CALORIE}\\ \text{FROM FAT}\end{array}$$

(Example: $\dfrac{8 \times 9}{310} = \dfrac{72}{310} = 22\%$)

Hard covers. Easy prices

For any occasion, few gifts are as enduring as Pillsbury's Best-selling Cookbooks.